Bitcoin vs. Banks

Bitcoin vs. Banks

Who Will Own the Future of Money?

Mateo Quiral

Mindful Pages

Published in 2026

ISBN: 9789374595701 (PB)
ISBN: 9789374590669 (eBook)

Published by

Mindful Pages
Imprint of Alpha Editions LLC
312 W. 2nd St #1834
Casper, WY 82601, USA

This book was developed using advanced writing tools to support the drafting and ideation process. All content has been thoughtfully curated, refined, and reviewed to ensure quality and relevance.

Content

Introduction

Picture a street vendor in Lagos, tapping a cheap smartphone against a customer's device to complete a sale. The signal travels at the speed of light, yet the money itself—once it enters the traditional pipes of commerce—slows to the speed of paperwork. Hours can pass before the vendor can pay a supplier. Days before the funds become "real." Trust must be checked manually, stamped and approved by institutions whose origins lie in a world of ink, vaults, and bankers' hours. Our payment technologies have raced ahead; our monetary plumbing remains stuck in a queue of intermediaries.

Or imagine a retiree in London who has saved for decades, only to watch elected officials, market sentiment, and unseen central bank committees determine the future purchasing power of their life's work. The numbers in their account never change form. Yet their meaning—what they can command in the real world—can shift overnight. The promise of stability hides a more uncomfortable truth: money is a political institution before it is a technological one.

Now consider a different kind of scene. An anonymous message posted to a mailing list in 2008. No authority, no fanfare, just an idea: a peer-to-peer electronic cash system. Something that could settle value without asking permission from any bank, government, or clearinghouse. Within months, computers around the world began agreeing on a shared ledger, verifying history not through trusted intermediaries but through computation itself. It was a strange and audacious proposition: rules without rulers; money without the mint.

This book is about the clash between those worlds. On one side, the incumbent architecture of money—central banks, commercial banks, payment networks—systems that have grown into towering institutions capable of steering nations and shaping geopolitical power. On the other, a cryptographic upstart—Bitcoin—which proposes that monetary trust can be engineered in code instead of enforced through hierarchy. Each claims to offer the foundation for economic life in the digital age. Only one can own the future of money, unless the future itself is more complicated than the question suggests.

For more than a century, the project of modern central banking has been a wager: allow a small cadre of experts to control the supply and integrity of money and the result will be stability, growth, and fairness. Sometimes, the wager pays off. Inflation is tamed. Crises are contained. Lenders of last resort prevent chaos from engulfing society. Yet history is littered with the debris of times when those guardians miscalculated or misjudged the priorities of the public. In 2008, the system did not break—it was saved—but the rescue redefined who bore the costs and who enjoyed the immunity. The aftershocks still reverberate: stagnant wages, asset inflation, political distrust. The scaffolding of legitimacy creaks under its own weight.

Bitcoin emerged from that moment not as a speculative toy, though it has certainly played that role, but as a protest. Its code encodes a moral judgement: that the authority to create and allocate money should not be confined to institutions prone to crisis and influenced by politics. Instead, the system would reward those who contribute security and discipline those who misbehave, not through fines, decrees, or legal action, but through math. It proposes a return to scarcity—a digital good that cannot be conjured at will—yet adapted for a borderless world.

At heart, this is not a battle between old and new technologies. It is a confrontation between two philosophies of monetary governance. Banks operate on a model of managed confidence: deposits promise instant withdrawal though money is always elsewhere; loans multiply claims on the same reserves; liquidity depends on belief never faltering. When it does falter, the state intervenes, picking winners and imposing losses, redefining the social contract in real time. Bitcoin's philosophy rejects the very premise. Finality is absolute, not promised. Ownership is direct, not delegated. There are no bailouts, no emergency meetings, no appeals to authority. The system does not negotiate; it executes.

Yet the story is not one of naïve decentralists against calculating centralists. Both systems have virtues born from necessity and flaws baked into their design. Banks excel at connecting savers with borrowers, expanding credit and enabling enterprise. Without them, industrialisation and much of the modern economy would never have materialised. Central banks provide a public good by defending the currency during turmoil, maintaining payments stability, and curbing inflation when it threatens livelihoods. Their legitimacy rests on empirical success, not divine mandate, and their task is extraordinarily complex.

Bitcoin, for its part, is radically transparent and resistant to censorship. It empowers individuals in places where currency collapses or governments weaponise finance. It offers a safe harbour in a world of monetary storms. But it also introduces new risks: losing a password can erase wealth forever; volatility tests the resolve of holders; and energy usage sparks fierce debate about costs and priorities. The network invites responsibility many are not prepared to shoulder. Freedom demands competence.

The friction between these paradigms is not merely academic. It shapes the daily lives of billions, determining who may transact, who may save, and under what conditions. It defines the boundary between public oversight and private autonomy. It influences whether financial power centralises further or disperses into the hands of citizens. And as our economies digitise, these questions grow sharper. Data flows do not respect borders. Payments increasingly depend on a handful of global firms. The more seamless the experience for users, the greater the concentration of influence among infrastructure providers.

This book examines that tension with clarity and intent. We begin by tracing how monetary power emerged: how rulers turned coins into instruments of governance; how gold's discipline gave way to policy discretion; how crises revealed the underlying politics of stability. We explore how banking evolved from merchants' ledgers into a system so large that governments are compelled to protect it at all costs. Then, we study Bitcoin not as a speculative chart but as a constitutional experiment—an attempt to design monetary rules that no one can unilaterally change.

Throughout, we will return to a metaphor: money as infrastructure, like the railways that transformed nineteenth-century commerce. The first rail lines were chaotic, privately built, and incompatible. Over time, consolidation led to efficiency—but also oligopoly. The same forces threaten digital value. The question is whether this time we can choose a different trajectory.

We will also widen the frame. Money is not experienced the same in every postcode. A stable currency in Frankfurt means something very different to a rapidly devaluing one in Buenos Aires. In countries where remittances are a lifeline, fees and delays erode opportunity. In places where banking access is a privilege, keys and phones may offer inclusion previously denied. The stakes of monetary design are not abstract; they decide who can participate in the global economy and who remains on the margins.

As institutions respond to Bitcoin's rise, battle lines shift. Corporations accumulate digital assets to hedge uncertainty. Asset managers and custodians build new products that promise convenience yet risk recapturing control. Regulators scramble to apply frameworks designed for intermediaries to systems built to minimise them. International coordination becomes strained as each jurisdiction weighs innovation against sovereignty. We are not just witnessing a technological transformation—this is a contest over governance, values, and the character of economic citizenship.

The core question is deceptively simple: who do we trust to define and guarantee the meaning of money? A technocratic institution guided by experts? A decentralised network governed by code? A hybrid model yet to be invented? Ultimately, the choice is not binary. The future may blend elements of both traditions. Deposit accounts could clear through cryptographic rails. Wallets might integrate protections without reintroducing coercive control. Citizens could hold their own keys while institutions offer services rather than supremacy.

But such outcomes are not inevitable. Power has a way of reasserting itself. Protocols built to decentralise can be repurposed into instruments of surveillance or exclusion. Networks intended to empower individuals can drift into new hierarchies, controlled by the few who operate gateways, validators, or regulatory mechanisms. The architecture of money embeds political assumptions, whether acknowledged or obscured. If we do not understand those assumptions, we risk sleepwalking into a future where digital convenience masks profound loss of agency.

That is why examining monetary systems matters now more than ever. As cash declines, privacy becomes a privilege. As payments consolidate, the potential for censorship expands. As inflation resurfaces, confidence erodes. The institutions that stabilised the twentieth century may not suffice for the challenges of the twenty-first: climate stress, geopolitical fragmentation, demographic shifts, and the automation of economic life. We stand at a monetary crossroads, not because Bitcoin demands our attention, but because the world it critiques is already changing beneath our feet.

This book does not offer investment tips, partisan cheerleading, or technological mystique. It asks the reader to think deeply about the foundations of economic freedom. What should money protect? Who should it empower? What rights accompany the responsibilities of ownership? And what forms of governance best uphold those values in a hyperconnected world? By the final chapter, the goal is not to declare a victor in the Bitcoin versus banks debate, but to equip you with the analytical tools to see through narratives and follow incentives to their logical ends.

The future of money will be shaped by choices—individual, institutional, and collective. Some will favour continuity, trusting banks and states to adapt. Others will embrace new protocols that shift authority to the edges of the network. Many will inhabit both worlds, hedging uncertainty with pluralism. What matters is not picking a tribe, but understanding the trade-offs. Stability is not free. Autonomy is not easy. Efficiency is not neutral.

We are invited to participate, not merely observe. To demand transparency rather than assuming benevolence. To test exit options instead of accepting defaults. To treat monetary fluency as a civic skill, not a specialist domain reserved for experts. The struggle over the future of money is already underway, and none of us are bystanders. We are the stakeholders, the counterparts, the end users whose preferences and behaviour will determine which model prevails.

So let us begin with open eyes and engaged minds. The stakes are nothing less than how value, trust, and sovereignty will operate in the digital age. The institutions of yesterday believe they deserve to rule tomorrow. The networks of tomorrow argue they can do better. The contest is not just about technology or policy. It is about what we, as societies and as individuals, choose to trust—and why.

Chapter 1
The Invention of Monetary Power

On a frigid morning in the winter of 1797, the Royal Mint's presses hammered relentlessly while news swept through London like a chill. Britain, locked in war with Revolutionary France, was running out of gold. Citizens queued anxiously outside the Bank of England, clutching banknotes they no longer trusted. They wanted metal—heavy, tangible, sovereign—before the state's promises collapsed into mere ink. But the gold coffers had run thin. The government ordered the suspension of convertibility, declaring that banknotes alone must suffice. In that moment, something profound happened: money was revealed not as a natural feature of the world but as a political construction, sustained by confidence and power rather than metal alone.

This tension between matter and mandate, between the glint of coin and the authority of the crown, is the original theatre of monetary power. Behind every token of value lies a struggle over who may define it. From ancient emperors quietly shaving precious metal from their coinage to modern policymakers steering entire economies by adjusting interest rates, rulers have long recognised that the authority to issue money is also the authority to shape society. Control the mint, and one controls not merely trade, but trust.

Yet this control has never been absolute. The legitimacy of currency must be constantly earned. When the metal content of coins dropped too far, riots flared. When the public suspected corruption, markets unraveled. Sovereigns learned quickly that their power over money depended upon managing the delicate equilibrium between confidence and compulsion. Every debasement risked rebellion; every tight constraint risked stagnation. The mint was a workshop of political limits.

Fast forward to the present and the symbols have changed—polymer notes, digital balances, central bank statements—but the stakes remain the same. Monetary power, once hammered into silver and gold, now resides in spreadsheets, committee rooms, and arcane policy frameworks. And still it determines who prospers, who struggles, and whose claims on the future are honoured or erased. Money has always been more than a medium of exchange; it is a social contract codified through authority.

This chapter explores that authority—how it emerged, how it evolved, and how it is contested each time crisis shakes the foundations of trust. We begin with the ancient logic of seigniorage: the alchemy by which rulers finance themselves through the currency they decree. Coinage allowed states to project reach across their territories. A monarch's face stamped into metal became both economic conduit and political message: *this is what power looks like; this is what value means.* A king with a mint could raise armies and build infrastructure. A king without one was merely a feudal landlord.

But the temptations were strong. Reduce the silver in the coin, and one could pay soldiers twice without raising taxes. Clip the edges, and the treasury grew. Yet subjects noticed when their money felt lighter than it used to. Debasement became a gamble of legitimacy—cheap victories today could cost the crown its credibility tomorrow. The metal standard placed a constraint on power but also forced transparency: authority could only stretch as far as the metal reserves allowed.

Then modernity intervened. Industrial economies demanded more flexibility than gold could offer. Economic life became too complex, too interconnected, too dependent on credit to be bound by fixed convertibility. Gradually, nations shifted from gold-backed assurance to institution-backed credibility. We trust money not because it can be melted into something useful, but because we trust the architects of monetary stability—central banks—to manage its value responsibly.

Yet this transition did not depoliticise money. It intensified the politics, now disguised as technocracy. Central banks present themselves as independent guardians—scientific, objective, immune to political pressure. Their independence, however, is hedged by democratic accountability on one side and state interests on the other. When public anger rises over inflation, housing affordability, or inequality, the central bank becomes a lightning rod. Its decisions reverberate through every mortgage contract and every pension fund balance sheet. The shift from gold to governance simply changed the kind of legitimacy demanded: from metallic certainty to institutional trust.

Trust, of course, tends to disappear precisely when it is most needed. Crises reveal the true priorities embedded in monetary systems. When panic strikes and bank queues spill down the block, the façade of stability dissolves. The state steps in as rescuer—printing, lending, guaranteeing—to stop a liquidity shortage from becoming a political catastrophe. Emergency actions redefine fairness in real time: which banks are saved, which companies fail, which savers lose everything. Monetary power turns visible and raw. Democracy finds itself in the queue, waiting to see who gets served.

Consider a simple scene: a community bank in distress. A whisper of insolvency; a sudden surge of withdrawals; managers pleading for calm. The people have lost confidence, and in banking, confidence *is* the business model. Only the state's guarantee can restore it. When governments promise to save depositors, they simultaneously endorse certain institutions as indispensable. *Too big to fail* becomes less a diagnosis than a declaration of political priority. Those outside the circle of protection learn the harsh lesson that money's safety is conditional and hierarchy-laden. Who is saved, and who is sacrificed, becomes a shorthand for the social contract's hidden clauses.

Underneath all of this lie the rails—the infrastructure that allows money to travel. Payments networks emerged in the nineteenth century much like railroads: fragmented at first, competitive and messy. Over time, consolidation brought uniformity and reach, but also dominance by those who controlled the switches. Clearinghouses, standards bodies, and private networks grew into natural monopolies. Efficiency demanded centralisation; innovation often suffered for it. The financial equivalent of railway barons learned that if you can control movement, you can control markets. Banks expanded their reach not only by issuing credit but by owning the very tracks on which commerce must run.

Even today, the railways of money remain largely invisible to the public. Tap a card, swipe a screen, send a payment across continents—these acts feel instant and effortless. But behind the interface lies a system defined by controlled entry, hierarchy, and gatekeeping. Small institutions must interconnect through larger ones. New entrants struggle to bypass entrenched toll-collectors. Network power concentrates over time. And when a technical glitch or policy directive halts the tracks, entire populations find themselves stuck. The convenience masks dependence.

Understanding how we arrived here requires refusing to view money as neutral. It is not a mere lubricant for trade but a lever of organisation and a form of governance. From the first stamped coin to the latest central bank digital currency proposal, each evolution in monetary design has reshaped society's structure of power. Who issues money? Who allocates credit? Who decides its value? Each answer has produced distinct winners and losers.

This chapter challenges the reader to look beyond the comforting abstraction of numbers in accounts and instead confront money as a political artefact. It asks us to see seigniorage as a form of taxation, central banking as a balancing act between autonomy and state need, crisis response as a window into the priorities of the social order, and payments infrastructure as a quiet custodian of inequality or inclusion.

The stakes are not confined to history books. As our world becomes more digital, the leverage of those who operate monetary systems grows larger. The institutions that once promised neutrality now sit at the centre of debates about privacy, access, and democracy. Calls for reform grow louder: should money be more public, less political, or more decentralised? Should financial infrastructure behave like a utility or a marketplace? Should central banks retain their privileged role or concede some authority to networks governed by code?

Those questions may feel modern, yet they echo ancient truths. Authority over money has always been authority over the future. A ruler who can reshape the currency can reshape society. A network that circumvents that ruler changes what sovereignty means.

As we proceed, we will excavate the layers of monetary power from their earliest foundations to their current expressions. We will walk the corridors of wartime mints and the glass towers of contemporary central banks. We will examine moments where confidence crumbled and new orders emerged. And we will scrutinise the pipes through which trillions flow daily, unnoticed but indispensable.

This is not merely a tour of financial architecture. It is an inquiry into legitimacy itself. Why do we trust money? Whose interests does that trust serve? When systems falter, who holds the authority to rewrite the rules? By the end of this chapter, we will see how the DNA of monetary power—control, credibility, crisis management, and infrastructure—

continues to shape the choices that lie ahead in the contest between banks and Bitcoin.

Turn the page and follow the trail of currency through history's crucibles. To understand where money may go next, we must first understand how power came to shape every coin, every note, and every digital unit of value we use today.

Seigniorage and Sovereigns

On 24 February 1797, the British government halted the convertibility of paper notes into gold as war with France drained the Bank of England's reserves. At the Tower Hill Mint in London, presses clattered through the night. Soldiers guarded deliveries of silver from Madrid and the Americas while newly minted coins poured into barrels stamped with the Crown. Panic outside subsided only when people believed the sovereign's promise: this token, though lighter than a year ago, still counted as full value. A nation at war was learning a lesson as old as coinage itself: control the currency and one controls both the battlefield and belief. Money was not merely metal. It was authority struck into circles of trust.

For as long as states have existed, rulers have recognised that the right to issue money is the right to tax without asking. *Seigniorage*—the profit made from creating currency at lower cost than its face value—was the quiet engine of governance. When Edward I of England reformed the penny in 1279, he standardised the silver content and centralised minting in the Tower of London. Merchants gained stable trade; the Crown gained a dependable revenue stream. Every coin carried not only value but messaging: the monarch's likeness, a declaration of legitimacy embedded in everyday exchange. A penny in the market was a piece of the sovereign in hand.

But stability was fragile. Over centuries, rulers struggled against a temptation that returned with every budget crisis or military campaign. Shave a sliver of silver from the coin, and suddenly the treasury grows without raising taxes. Replace silver with copper beneath thin plating, and soldiers march another season. In 1544, Henry VIII of England began a notorious debasement, reducing the silver in the shilling from over 90 per cent to barely one-third by 1551. Prices rose. Foreign merchants demanded higher rates to accept English coins. The King was mocked as "Old Coppernose," the portrait on the coin rubbing away to reveal base metal beneath. The mint had funded war, but at the cost of reputation.

The motif is simple, recurring, and revealing: weight matters. When a coin feels lighter, so does the sovereign's promise.

A different example: in 1680s France, Louis XIV entrusted his finance minister Jean-Baptiste Colbert with filling the coffers. Colbert increased minting, replaced foreign coins, and extracted profit from the spread between metal content and official value. Paris prospered briefly. But repeated tampering eroded confidence. By 1709, war and fiscal stress forced a drastic recoinage, fuelling public unrest. French historian Françoise Bayard (1991) documented how Parisians distrusted royal money so deeply that bread riots broke out when newly issued coins circulated. Legitimacy could not be minted on demand.

Not every sovereign succumbed to the easy outrage of reducing metal. The Ming dynasty's attempt to issue paper currency in the fourteenth century offers a counter-example. At first, *Da Ming Baochao* notes, backed by decree rather than metal, facilitated internal trade across vast distances. But the temptations of seigniorage persisted: over-issuance caused inflation and collapse by the mid-fifteenth century. The absence of intrinsic value required even greater discipline than silver or gold. It was not forthcoming. The lesson reconciles the contradiction: whether metallic or paper, money derives value from shared confidence in the issuer's restraint. Without it, even innovation becomes liability.

Seen across continents and centuries, one principle remains constant: monetary power is fiscal power. When the Thirty Years' War engulfed central Europe (1618–1648), states facing ruin turned to the mint as survival strategy. The Kipper und Wipper inflation in German states around 1620 saw coins consistently clipped and reissued with diminished metal. The practice financed troops but destroyed trade. Cities recorded starvation deaths. Trust in currency vanished so completely that barter returned. This crisis confirmed what rulers preferred to forget: debasement is not a policy tool; it is a countdown.

The mechanics may be ancient, yet the logic persists—only the materials have changed. In 1914, when Britain entered the First World War, the Treasury issued paper currency known as Bradbury notes, named after Sir John Bradbury, the official signer. Gold coins disappeared from circulation. Again, weight vanished; authority remained. The government financed unprecedented military expenditure through borrowing and controlled issuance. Citizens continued to exchange paper because the state guaranteed redemption—later. A century after Henry VIII, the strategy was cleaner, the trust more institutional, but the underlying truth identical: wartime money is a political artefact.

This interplay between necessity and legitimacy is the quiet motif of monetary history. Rulers mint coins to finance defence, but they must preserve belief; once belief erodes, even the strongest armies can find themselves paid in worthless metal. Sovereignty over money therefore demands performance on two fronts: resource extraction and confidence maintenance. Formal taxation is difficult and resented. Seigniorage is discreet and effective, until it is not.

By the nineteenth century, industrialising economies stretched the limits of coinage. Credit expanded. Commerce accelerated. Money needed to scale without dependence on physical commodities. Central banks arose to coordinate issuance across markets rather than mints alone. The Bank of England's influence after the 1844 Bank Charter Act formalised a shift: policy could adjust supply more subtly than stamping metal ever could. Convertibility into gold remained on paper, but in practice, credibility rested increasingly on the institution's stewardship. The sovereign's face faded from coins; authority migrated into the signatures of bankers.

This transition from the weight of metal to the weight of governance did not eliminate the power dynamics—it concealed them. Political scientist Hyman Minsky observed in 1986 that every financial innovation reintroduced old vulnerabilities in new wrapping. Central banking preserved the monarchy's fiscal prerogatives while adding a layer of expert management. Seigniorage continued, now through inflation rather than debasement. When the money supply grows faster than economic output, the state captures value invisibly. Citizens pay without noticing. The analogue to clipped coinage is a shrinking purchasing power.

A pattern emerges: crises expose the architecture of control. During the Great Depression, Franklin D. Roosevelt nationalised gold in the United States in 1933, fixing its price and outlawing private possession above small thresholds. The justification was national recovery; the result was a transfer of monetary power to Washington. Citizens holding paper had no choice but to accept whatever value the government assigned. Once more, sovereignty recalibrated weight into will.

Because money is also messaging, seigniorage remains ideological. When the euro was introduced in 2002, replacing national currencies across twelve European states, its notes omitted portraits of politicians or monarchs. Bridges and windows appeared instead—symbols of openness and unity. Yet the European Central Bank, not any national treasury, now reaped the benefits of issuance. Citizens handled designs that speak of shared identity, while the underlying power centralised in Frankfurt. Legitimacy demanded harmony in imagery, even as fiscal tensions simmered beneath.

The tension is unresolved: if the state funds itself by creating money, how does it prevent excess? Economists like Thomas Sargent (1982) traced hyperinflation episodes—from Weimar Germany in 1923 to Zimbabwe in 2008—as failures of institutional constraint rather than metal shortage. Once trust breaks, numbers accelerate meaninglessly. People measure worth in bread loaves, not currency units. The coin, the note, the digital balance—none reassure. Only restored belief does.

As we advance further into the digital century, seigniorage has acquired new tools. Central banks manipulate interest rates, adjust balance sheets, and deploy quantitative easing to influence credit conditions. These are the twenty-first century's clipping shears. Instead of altering metal content, policymakers alter the money supply directly. The public rarely perceives the connection between an expansion of central bank reserves and its effect on everyday prices. The mint has become a database; power hides in balance sheets.

Yet the motif persists: weight, once literal, is now symbolic. We trust that central banks will maintain *value-weight*—the purchasing power embodied in money. When inflation spikes or institutions appear captured by political agendas, the ghost of debasement returns. Citizens ask, silently or aloud: *Is my money lighter than before?*

The 1797 presses at Tower Hill illustrate how these choices accumulate. The British government defended the pound with determination, promising eventual return to gold. They succeeded. Trust held. That episode became evidence that a state can suspend the weight of metal without suspending legitimacy. But not every state manages the balancing act. When Argentina's peso collapsed repeatedly between 2001 and 2023, printing funded short-term agendas while wiping out savings. The mint financed the state; citizens bore the cost.

Every system of seigniorage invites one central question: for whom is the currency sovereign? When debasement funds war, is it patriotic necessity or coercion cloaked in coin? When inflation funds stimulus, does it reflect democratic priorities or institutional convenience? When digital tools allow limitless issuance, who enforces restraint?

The image that threads through this story—the feel of a coin, its weight in the palm—reminds us that money has always signified more than price. It signals the reach of authority and the contours of consent. Whether etched in silver or encoded in policy statements, currency tells a political story: *you may trust this, and therefore you may trust us.*

That trust has a breaking point. Sovereigns throughout history have tested it, sometimes discovering the line only when revolt or collapse drew it sharp. Today's stewards of money will face the same boundary, even if the tokens they issue never weigh more than a few bytes. The mint remains a battleground of legitimacy. The question lingers every time the presses run faster: how much lighter can money become before belief falls through the fingers that hold it?

From Gold to Governance

On 15 August 1971, Richard Nixon addressed the American public from the White House. Flanked by advisers, he declared that the United States would "temporarily" suspend the dollar's convertibility into gold. It was a Sunday evening; the markets were closed. Yet the decision instantly severed the anchor that had moored the post-war monetary order. For the first time since the nineteenth century, the world's reserve currency could no longer be exchanged for a fixed amount of metal. The outcome, confirmed within days across capitals from London to Tokyo, was irreversible. Gold no longer set the limits of state power; credibility would have to replace it. A rule enforced by weight gave way to a rule enforced by judgement.

The Nixon Shock did not emerge from ideological frenzy but from arithmetic. By mid-1971, America's foreign liabilities exceeded its gold reserves at Fort Knox. Speculators and foreign governments requested redemption; the drain intensified. The guarantee that one ounce equalled thirty-five dollars—codified at Bretton Woods in 1944—had become untenable. The United States could defend the peg or defend its domestic priorities. It could not do both. Nixon chose to preserve the latter, and the world transitioned to a system where the value of money rested on institutional credibility rather than metal scarcity. A five-word sentence captures the shift. The anchor was gone.

The motif of the *anchor* threads through every phase of this transformation. Gold had been a literal anchor: heavy, finite, difficult to manipulate. Its constraints forced governments to align ambition with reserves. But it was also a political anchor, signalling restraint. When convertibility disappeared, policymakers needed a new form of ballast. Central banks stepped into that role, claiming independence as their substitute for metal. Credibility would be earned through actions rather than coin.

The shift to governance was not abrupt; it was the culmination of decades in which gold's authority eroded. One example stands out. When Britain suspended gold convertibility in August 1914, days after entering the First World War, the Treasury issued Treasury Notes and encouraged citizens to "pay with paper." The gold window closed at the Bank of England on Threadneedle Street. Though initially presented as a wartime contingency, the suspension persisted until 1925. Chancellor Winston Churchill restored the gold standard that year at the pre-war parity of £4.86 per ounce. The visible behaviour—committing to a deflationary conversion rate despite domestic strain—reflected a belief that credibility could be reclaimed only by returning to metal. But the implication was severe: the economy endured contraction, unemployment rose, and the standard collapsed again in

1931. Credibility tethered too tightly to gold proved self-defeating.

A second example illustrates the opposite dynamic. In 1933, Franklin D. Roosevelt ordered all private gold in the United States to be surrendered to the Federal Reserve, signing Executive Order 6102. Gold ownership was restricted; convertibility abolished. The dollar was then devalued from $20.67 to $35 per ounce under the Gold Reserve Act of 1934. The visible decision—removing metal from public hands—signalled a break with orthodoxy. Roosevelt judged that recovery required monetary discretion. The implication was transformative: governments could expand money supply without defending a fixed parity. Gold lost its primacy as a public constraint; institutional policy became the new foundation for value.

These cases show that gold, once revered as a neutral arbiter, was increasingly incompatible with economies built on credit, speed, and political choice. Convertibility forced governments to prioritise external promises over domestic welfare. When crises struck, metal discipline revealed its limits. Countries like France, which clung to gold longer during the interwar period (holding large reserves in Paris through the late 1920s), enjoyed temporary strength but contributed to global deflationary pressures identified by economists Barry Eichengreen and Peter Temin (1997). Persistence in gold became a form of rigidity. The anchor held, but the ship listed dangerously.

The counter-example is equally instructive. Switzerland maintained a partial gold backing for its franc well into the late twentieth century; until 1999, the Swiss National Bank was legally required to hold at least 40 per cent gold reserves. This constraint appeared to preserve stability, and the franc remained widely trusted. Yet the limitation eventually clashed with the scale of global capital flows and Switzerland's integration into modern financial markets. In 1999, the country amended its constitution to end the requirement. The reconciliation lies in recognising that metal can signal virtue but cannot manage complexity. Even disciplined states must adapt when the anchor impedes navigation.

Once gold's grip loosened, independence became the successor doctrine. The modern central bank presented itself as neutral guardian, insulated from politics by statutory design. The Bundesbank embodied this model. After its creation in 1957, it earned a reputation for strict anti-inflation policy, guided by an institutional culture shaped by Germany's memory of the 1923 hyperinflation. Its behaviour—raising interest rates even when governments protested—signalled commitment to price stability above electoral convenience. The implication was a powerful one: credibility could be constructed through consistent action rather than metallic backing.

Yet claims of independence have always been fragile. Politics surrounds central banks even as statutes constrain them. Consider the Federal Reserve during the 1951 Accord with the U.S. Treasury. In the preceding decade, the Fed had capped government bond yields to support wartime financing. By 1951, inflation demanded tighter policy. The Accord restored the Fed's authority to adjust rates, but only after tense negotiations between Chairman Thomas McCabe, Treasury Secretary John Snyder, and President Harry Truman. The visible behaviour—public disagreement, private compromise—exposed the reality that independence is negotiated, not absolute. The Fed gained operational space but remained bound to political expectations.

The European Central Bank adds another layer to the motif. When it began operating in Frankfurt in 1998, the ECB inherited the Bundesbank's culture but expanded it across a continent. Its mandate was narrow—price stability—and its independence protected by treaty. Yet during the eurozone crisis in 2012, President Mario Draghi's commitment to "do whatever it takes" created a political moment as potent as any parliamentary vote. Bond yields in Italy and Spain fell sharply within days of the pledge. The behaviour was technical—an announcement of conditional bond purchases—but the implication unmistakable: the ECB could determine the survival of member states through expectations alone. Independence became a theatre of power.

The motif reappears here. The anchor is no longer gold; it is perception. Policymakers measure credibility by market reactions. Bond spreads, inflation expectations, and currency movements become the new weights. The judgment of traders replaces the rigidity of metal. But while markets can discipline excess, they cannot eliminate the political stakes. When a central bank raises interest rates to control inflation, mortgage holders see costs rise, companies cut investment, and governments face higher debt servicing. Credibility has a price.

The transition from convertibility to governance reshaped how states communicate value. Under gold, the behaviour was literal: present bullion, receive redemption. Under governance, the behaviour is institutional: publish forecasts, adjust policy rates, manage balance sheets. Yet the implication for citizens is unchanged. Money depends on trust in the steward. Only the steward has changed.

The shift also redefined failure. Under gold, a run on reserves signalled impending collapse. Under governance, failure manifests differently: inflation drifting above target, bond markets refusing to buy sovereign debt, or political movements accusing central banks of overreach. In September 1992, Britain's ejection from the Exchange Rate Mechanism after George Soros bet against the pound demonstrated this vividly. The Bank of England raised interest rates twice in one day, up to 15 per cent, yet failed to defend the currency. The visible metric—reserve depletion—revealed that credibility without adequate capacity falters. Governance requires tools; belief alone is insufficient.

Still, governance offers advantages that gold never did. It allows states to respond to crises with flexibility. During the 2008 global financial crisis, the Bank of England, under Governor Mervyn King, expanded its balance sheet and cut rates dramatically. Quantitative easing stabilised markets and prevented deeper contraction. The metal anchor would have forced austerity; governance enabled intervention. But intervention deepened entanglement: governments expected support, markets anticipated accommodation, and voters questioned why unelected officials held such sway. Independence shielded central banks from partisan pressure, yet it also shrouded them from democratic scrutiny.

The quiet tension running through all these examples is simple: who anchors whom? Do central banks anchor the state, or does the state anchor the central bank? Statutes grant independence, but parliaments write the statutes. Markets reward discipline, but only when it aligns with broader expectations. Citizens accept central bank authority, but only as long as outcomes—stable prices, functioning credit—justify it.

The present era amplifies these tensions. Inflation re-emerged across advanced economies in 2021–2023 after pandemic disruptions, energy shocks, and supply constraints. Central banks raised rates aggressively. The visible decisions—rate hikes of 50 or 75 basis points—revealed the governing philosophy: credibility must be defended even at the cost of slower growth. Yet elected governments faced pressure to protect households from rising rents and food prices. Independence and entanglement collided. The motif returns. The anchor must hold.

The legacy of the gold standard endures not in its metallic form but in its ideal: the promise of restraint. Modern governance substitutes institutional commitment for convertibility, but the demand for discipline remains. Citizens may no longer carry coins of precious metal, but they still feel the weight of monetary decisions in mortgages, wages, and savings. Each policy statement attempts to recreate what gold once provided automatically: a sense that the value of money will endure.

The unresolved question is whether credibility can continue to anchor monetary systems as effectively as gold once did. Central banks have formidable tools, but their mandates expand, their communication becomes politicised, and their interventions grow more frequent. The alternative—returning to metal—is impractical. The path forward requires a different test. When the anchor is trust rather than gold, how do societies measure its strength, and who decides when it begins to slip?

Crisis as Teacher

At 7:30 a.m. on 14 September 2007, customers gathered outside the Northern Rock branch on Northumberland Street in Newcastle. Some clutched umbrellas, others held thermos flasks, but all carried the same intent: withdraw their savings before the bank failed. By mid-morning, BBC cameras showed a queue stretching along the pavement. The faces were unmistakable—worried, impatient, resolute. The bank had received emergency liquidity from the Bank of England the previous day, but the revelation triggered panic rather than calm. Within forty-eight hours, Northern Rock lost more than 10 per cent of its retail deposits. A line in a rainy street became a referendum on the meaning of money. It exposed, in public view, the hierarchy of who gets protection and who waits in the cold.

A bank run always begins with a whisper: a rumour of losses, a leaked document, a late-night announcement. But it becomes political the moment people act. In Newcastle that morning, the visible behaviour—ordinary citizens queuing to reclaim their own money—measured the erosion of confidence more accurately than any spreadsheet. It forced the government to intervene. By 17 September 2007, Chancellor Alistair Darling guaranteed all existing Northern Rock deposits. The guarantee stopped the queues. It also rewrote assumptions about who would be saved when the system trembled. A single decision recast the social contract in real time. The state stepped forward; depositors stepped back from the brink.

The motif of the *queue* threads through every crisis. Who waits? Who bypasses the line? Who receives protection before panic even begins? Crashes reveal these answers with clarity that polite policy debates obscure.

A crisis teaches through exposure. It shows that banks operate on a knife-edge of maturity transformation; that deposits redeemable instantly are invested in assets that take time—sometimes years—to unwind. Northern Rock depended heavily on short-term wholesale markets. When these markets froze in August 2007, the bank's business model collapsed. The name matters. Wholesale funding—institutions lending to institutions—formed the foundation of Northern Rock's growth. When those lenders retreated, retail depositors saw the smoke. The implication was stark: modern bank runs begin in the interbank market long before they appear on high streets. The queue arrives last.

Another example demonstrates how quickly public order can turn into political crisis. When Lehman Brothers collapsed on 15 September 2008 in New York, the immediate victims were not retail savers but money market funds—vehicles assumed to be ultra-safe. The Reserve Primary Fund "broke the buck," meaning its net asset value fell below one dollar. Investors rushed to redeem. The visible metric—the fund's value dipping to 97 cents—shattered the illusion of stability. Within days, the U.S. Treasury created a temporary guarantee for money market funds, echoing the logic of Northern Rock but at a scale that encompassed global finance. The decision implied a hierarchy of rescue: markets essential to corporate funding would be prioritised before those affecting household deposits. The queue, once again, told the truth.

Crises also illuminate asymmetry. Some institutions receive lifelines before the public realises danger exists. Consider 2008 again. The Federal Reserve extended emergency credit to AIG on 16 September at terms designed to prevent systemic collapse. The behaviour—offering an $85 billion loan facility—signalled that certain firms sat within an inner circle of indispensability. AIG insured vast portfolios of mortgage-backed securities; its failure threatened the financial architecture itself. The implication was unavoidable: the system protects its own core before it protects individuals. The queue around Northern Rock snaked visibly through Newcastle streets; the queue around AIG was invisible, negotiated in conference rooms, but no less real.

One counter-example helps clarify the pattern by highlighting its exception. When Washington Mutual (WaMu) failed in September 2008, it did not receive a direct government bailout. Instead, regulators seized it and sold its assets to JPMorgan Chase. Depositors were protected, but equity and bondholders absorbed losses. The behaviour—swift regulatory intervention without extraordinary public guarantees—seemed to respect market discipline. Yet even here, the reconciliation shows that WaMu's failure, though the largest bank failure in U.S. history, posed fewer systemic linkages than AIG or Citigroup. The queue was rearranged, not abolished. Those whose failure threatened the architecture received protection. Those whose collapse could be contained did not.

The motif returns. Crises reorder the queue.

Crashes do more than reveal priorities; they redefine them. Emergency facilities—the alphabet soup of TAFs, TSLFs, and QE programmes—do not merely provide liquidity. They shift the boundaries of responsibility. The Bank of England's Special Liquidity Scheme launched in April 2008 allowed banks to swap illiquid mortgage-backed securities for government bonds. The behaviour was technical: asset swapping under strict collateral haircuts. But the implication was philosophical. The state signalled that stabilising balance sheets outranked adhering to the traditional separation between public and private risk. Liquidity became public infrastructure.

During the eurozone crisis, the European Central Bank's actions made this even more explicit. The Long-Term Refinancing Operations of 2011–2012 provided three-year loans to banks across the continent. Italy, Spain, and Portugal relied heavily on these facilities. The visible metric—over €1 trillion borrowed—showed the depth of dependence. Banks used ECB liquidity to buy their own countries' sovereign bonds, tightening the link between fiscal health and banking stability. Governance became circular. The implication was delicate: sovereigns stabilised banks, and banks stabilised sovereigns. Emergency measures redrew the contract binding state and financial sector.

Crises also escalate distributional consequences into view. In 1997–1998, during the Asian Financial Crisis, the IMF provided structural adjustment programmes to Thailand, Indonesia, and South Korea. The decisions—mandated fiscal tightening, interest rate hikes, and bank closures—exposed a tension between international conditionality and domestic welfare. While the programmes stabilised currencies, they also imposed severe social costs. The limitation stands out: emergency assistance is rarely neutral. It reflects the values and priorities of those who design it. The reconciliation lies in acknowledging that crisis management always chooses winners and losers. The queue extends across borders.

Some crises, however, show the limits of state rescue. In Argentina's 2001–2002 collapse, the government froze bank accounts through the *corralito*. Withdrawals were restricted. Streets filled with protests. Here, the visible behaviour—gates locked, signs posted limiting daily withdrawals to a few hundred pesos—revealed something different. The state, unable to guarantee deposits or currency value, protected the banking system by sacrificing depositor access. The motif darkens. The queue forms, but the doors stay shut. Emergency measures did not restore confidence; they replaced it with coercion.

Reconciling these cases demonstrates a central truth: every crisis teaches, but each lesson depends on institutional capacity. Northern Rock needed a guarantee. Lehman's aftermath required a reinvention of liquidity facilities. Argentina's collapse revealed the consequences when the state lacks the ability or credibility to intervene effectively. The queue—visible or metaphorical—shows the health of the social contract itself.

A quiet tension runs through all these episodes. Crashes expose hidden interdependencies. Depositors depend on banks; banks depend on markets; markets depend on central bank promises. Central banks, in turn, depend on political support. During the 2020 pandemic shock, central banks worldwide launched extraordinary interventions. The U.S. Federal Reserve's announcement on 23 March 2020 that it would buy corporate bonds—something unprecedented—calmed markets instantly. The visible metric was the collapse of credit spreads over the following week. The behaviour showed that central banks now acted as buyers of last resort. The implication was that the boundary of support had expanded again. Intervention became expectation.

The queue motif reappears: during the pandemic, large firms accessed bond markets within days. Small businesses waited weeks for government-backed loans. Individuals faced furlough schemes or income uncertainty while markets stabilised rapidly. Crisis response accelerated the divergence between those with direct access to institutional liquidity and those with only indirect access through political decisions.

Crises, then, function as diagnostic tools. They reveal the architecture of modern money more clearly than any policy document. They expose who has immediate claims on the state's balance sheet and who must rely on political rhetoric. They show that emergency facilities, though framed as temporary, often set precedents that reshape expectations long after the panic dissipates.

A question lingers beneath every example: what does fairness mean when stability is the overriding goal? Deposit guarantees prioritise households, but often only after wholesale markets have been secured. Bailouts protect institutions, but often at the cost of moral outrage. Restrictions like Argentina's *corralito* defend banks but betray savers. Each decision redraws the line between public and private risk.

As financial systems grow more interconnected and digital, the queue shortens in time but lengthens in consequence. Runs may occur not on high streets but via smartphones in seconds. Emergency facilities may need to operate faster and more broadly than ever before. Yet the underlying dilemma endures.

When the queue forms again—whether outside a branch in Newcastle, in the corridors of a finance ministry, or across a network of instant transfers—who will be allowed to bypass it, and who will be left waiting?

The Railways of Money

On 23 October 1861, a consortium of New York banks formed the New York Clearing House Association in a modest building on Pine Street. By the end of its first full day, clerks had exchanged and settled more than $22 million in cheques—an extraordinary sum for a country still fighting a civil war. The Clearing House eliminated the need for couriers to criss-cross Manhattan delivering bags of paper claims between banks. Instead, each institution sent a single representative to the same room. Sheets were tallied, imbalances netted, and settlement achieved before noon. What began as a simple logistical fix became a template. A private club of banks, meeting daily, built the railway tracks on which American money would run. The outcome was unmistakable: efficiency increased, but so did concentration. The rails served everyone, yet only a few controlled the switches.

The motif of *tracks*—quiet, rigid, and essential—runs through the history of payments. Once tracks are laid, commerce follows their path. They channel economic activity not by decree but by design. The more traffic they carry, the harder they are to replace.

The Clearing House also revealed something deeper. Its meeting hall was not a neutral room. It was an arena where membership conferred privilege. In 1873, when the panic struck, New York's major banks issued Clearing House Loan Certificates to settle obligations among themselves, while institutions outside the club scrambled for liquidity. The visible behaviour—members receiving immediate relief, outsiders waiting desperately—showed how infrastructure becomes hierarchy. Standards stabilised the system for those inside, yet constrained innovation for those left out.

A second example demonstrates how these dynamics travelled across borders. When the Bankers' Clearing House opened in London in 1810, it formalised a practice already honed by private bankers along Lombard Street. The central location allowed clerks from institutions like Barclays and Lloyds to exchange claims quickly. Over decades, manual entries evolved into mechanical processes and later into fully automated netting. Yet the governance structure barely changed. The largest clearing banks dominated rule-making. The outcome, confirmed repeatedly through the nineteenth century, was a system that reduced settlement risk while reinforcing incumbency. The clearinghouse acted like a junction station: anyone could travel the route, but timetables were written by those who owned the platforms.

A counter-example helps expose the pattern by highlighting its exception. In Sweden, the Riksbank introduced an early form of real-time settlement in the 1950s for interbank transfers, decades before comparable systems emerged elsewhere. The service—RIX in its modern form—reduced dependency on a private clearing cartel by placing the central bank in the role of neutral operator. Yet even this model did not eliminate concentration. Only licensed banks and a few large payment institutions could access RIX directly. The reconciliation appears in the architecture: technology can broaden access, but regulatory and operational requirements still gate entry. The tracks widen, yet the drivers remain few.

Payments networks, once established, behave like infrastructure because they demand coordination. Standards—routing codes, message formats, settlement times—produce certainty. Certainty begets adoption. Adoption strengthens incumbents. By the late twentieth century, two global card networks, Visa and Mastercard, connected tens of thousands of banks through proprietary rules that determined everything from interchange fees to fraud liabilities. The visible metric—market share—illustrated dominance: according to the Nilson Report (2023), the two networks accounted for more than 85 per cent of global card transaction volume outside China. Their growth was not accidental. It followed the logic of railways. A merchant accepts the card that consumers carry. Consumers carry the card most widely accepted. Tracks reinforce themselves.

Clearinghouses follow similar logic. SWIFT, founded in Brussels in 1973, standardised financial messaging across borders. Its early membership—239 banks from 15 countries—designed the protocols. Today more than 11,000 institutions rely on SWIFT for transfers. The behaviour—sending messages in a format defined by the cooperative—reinforces the motif: once a standard becomes universal, deviating from it becomes costly. Innovation at the edges slows because any new system must either interoperate with SWIFT or replace it. Few have the power to attempt either.

Efficiency often hides the trade-offs. Faster settlement reduces credit risk. Netting decreases liquidity demands. But these benefits accrue unevenly. After the 2008 crisis, central banks introduced new infrastructures such as the Federal Reserve's Fedwire modernisation (2012) and the Bank of England's CHAPS reforms (2017). These systems improved resilience. Yet direct participation remained limited to institutions meeting high capital, operational, and supervisory standards. The visible decision—restricting membership to protect stability—meant smaller banks and fintechs depended on larger intermediaries for access. In infrastructure terms, they could travel the tracks, but only by buying a ticket from those who held the licences.

The motif returns. Ownership of the tracks shapes who moves.

Standards can empower or constrain. The adoption of ISO 20022—a unified messaging standard—offers a recent illustration. Implemented by major payment systems beginning in 2023, the standard promises richer data fields and greater harmonisation. But harmonisation also centralises control. The institutions participating in shaping the standard, like the European Central Bank and the Federal Reserve, determine its evolution. The behaviour—joint committees drafting message specifications—shows how governance remains tied to the largest operators. The implication is clear: future innovation will depend on compatibility with rules written by a small cadre of technical stewards.

Clearinghouses also demonstrate how risk can be redistributed silently. During the 2010 "Flash Crash," when U.S. equity markets plunged briefly, clearing institutions increased margin requirements sharply. The immediate behaviour—raising collateral calls—exposed the power of rule-setting. Brokers and traders had little choice but to comply. The implication extends beyond markets: a similar mechanism operates in payments. When clearinghouses adjust collateral requirements for banks, the costs ripple through lending, liquidity, and credit availability. Infrastructure decisions become economic signals.

Yet there are moments when infrastructure expands rather than entrenches. India's Unified Payments Interface (UPI), launched by the National Payments Corporation of India in 2016, offers a partial counterpoint. By enabling instant, low-cost transfers between banks and fintech apps, UPI reduced reliance on card networks for domestic payments. The behaviour—hundreds of millions of monthly transactions—demonstrated the impact of open access. But the limitation is instructive. UPI succeeded because a state-backed entity coordinated standards and provided centralised switching. The reconciliation lies in understanding that even disruptive infrastructure relies on central control. Tracks may be free to use, but a single operator still directs the flow of trains.

The structure of payments networks mirrors the logic of all infrastructure: high fixed costs, strong network effects, and political sensitivity. When the Faster Payments Service launched in the United Kingdom in 2008, it allowed near-instant transfers. Yet for years, direct access was confined to a handful of large banks. Smaller players depended on agency banks to connect. This meant that innovation in consumer-facing apps and fintech services ultimately flowed through pipes owned by incumbents. The behaviour—queues of firms seeking indirect access—measured how infrastructure restricts contestability. The implication is a constraint on competition even as technical capability expands.

This tension becomes sharper as payments migrate to digital wallets and mobile platforms. Apple Pay and Google Pay illustrate a new pattern: infrastructure sits not only in banks and central banks but also in consumer devices. The decision by Apple to restrict near-field communication (NFC) access on iPhones has been the subject of regulatory scrutiny in the EU since 2020. The behaviour—limiting which apps can process contactless payments—demonstrates that gatekeeping can shift from clearinghouses to technology firms. The motif persists. Tracks change shape, but the switches remain in few hands.

Crises expose the fragility of these networks. When Visa suffered a widespread outage across Europe on 1 June 2018, millions of card transactions failed. Shops displayed handwritten "cash only" signs. The visible behaviour—queues forming at cash machines, staff manually noting card details for later reconciliation—brought the infrastructure's invisibility into sharp relief. The outage stemmed from a hardware failure, but its implication was systemic: a single point of failure disrupted commerce across dozens of countries. Railways do not tolerate broken tracks.

These networks also become instruments of policy. In 2012, as sanctions tightened on Iran, several Iranian banks were disconnected from SWIFT under EU regulation. The behaviour—removing access to the global messaging network—demonstrated how infrastructure embeds geopolitical power. Payments rails enforce borders more effectively than many laws. The implication is unambiguous: whoever controls the railways of money controls participation itself.

Innovation that challenges these rails often finds itself slowed by the weight of accumulated standards. Attempts to introduce real-time cross-border systems, such as the Bank of England's exploratory work with the Bank for International Settlements (2021–2023), confront the reality that interoperability requires coordination across legal systems, technical standards, and competing national priorities. The behaviour—pilot projects, limited-scale testing—shows progress, but the implication remains: replacing global tracks is harder than building new ones.

The queue motif reappears in a new form. Who gets to connect directly to the rails, and who must depend on intermediaries? Who sets the rules that define the cost and speed of moving money? Who has a voice in designing the standards that carry trillions each day?

As payments networks evolve, the most important question persists. If money now moves on tracks laid by a handful of institutions—public, private, or hybrid—what happens when the next innovation demands new paths? Who decides whether the tracks will bend, or whether everyone must continue travelling along routes built decades ago?

Chapter 2
Bitcoin: A Stateless Money

A man sits at his kitchen table in Singapore, staring at a slip of paper with 12 seemingly random words. They are his only key to a sum of money large enough to change his life. No bank holds the funds. No customer helpline can help if he forgets. In that fragile cipher lies the most radical departure Bitcoin offers: value that exists without the permission or protection of any institution. Lose the key, lose the money. Keep the key, and sovereignty is yours.

For most of human history, money has been a story of trust delegated—trust in banks to honour deposits, trust in governments to protect currency, trust in systems that can be appealed to when something goes wrong. Bitcoin reverses the burden. It proposes a daring question: what if trust could be embedded in software itself? What if the rules of money did not bend to emergencies, elections, or geopolitics, but operated with the same implacable regularity as mathematics?

This chapter explores that proposition. Bitcoin is often caricatured as speculation, ideology, or mere digital novelty. Yet its true challenge is deeper: it reimagines the foundation of monetary authority. Where traditional money relies on institutions to enforce scarcity and ownership, Bitcoin distributes those guarantees across strangers connected by code. Where banks grant access contingent on compliance and creditworthiness, Bitcoin treats every participant as sovereign by default. Where central banking relies on policy judgement and intervention, Bitcoin depends on consensus engineered into infrastructure. It is a constitutional experiment disguised as software.

Consider the question of scarcity. In previous eras, scarcity came from nature: gold must be mined; land is finite. Bitcoin manufactures scarcity through physics-bound computation.

Proof-of-work transforms electricity and time into cryptographic security, allowing the network to decide together which transactions are legitimate. Blocks of transactions are discovered, not assigned. Difficulty adjusts to maintain a steady rhythm: approximately one block every ten minutes, regardless of how many machines compete. This cadence acts as a public clock—one the world winds collectively. And every four years, the clock ticks into a new era as the block subsidy halves, slowing the creation of new coins until the total reaches 21 million. Unlike central banks, Bitcoin does not ask the public to trust that issuance will remain controlled. It commits to the limitation in code. The metaphor that lingers is geological: Bitcoin is digital gold with a predictable vein.

But scarcity means little without ownership. And ownership in Bitcoin is radical in its simplicity: possession of private keys equals control of funds. There are no accounts in the banking sense—no profiles that can be frozen, reversed, or audited without consent. Bitcoins are bearer instruments. They embody a return to property in its most literal form: what is yours is whatever you can sign for. Yet such autonomy carries risk. Keys lost to a discarded hard drive or forgotten password vanish from circulation. There are countless tales of Bitcoin fortunes irretrievable, each a reminder that sovereignty and support are opposites. That tension has driven the rise of custodians, exchanges, and wallet services—intermediaries that reintroduce trust for those unwilling or unprepared to hold it alone. Bitcoin invites self-reliance, but the practical world often negotiates a hybrid.

Coordination is equally essential. A money without governance would descend quickly into chaos. Bitcoin prevents this through incentives that align participants' behaviour. Miners commit resources to secure the ledger, receiving rewards and fees in return. Full nodes independently validate rules, rejecting any block that violates consensus. Users signal support for upgrades by the software they choose to run. The system functions not through a hierarchy of authority but through a balance of power distributed across actors who need one another. When disagreement arises—over block size, privacy enhancements, or transaction ordering—forks become credible threats. Competing visions can split the network. The risk disciplines negotiators. No one controls Bitcoin, because everyone must agree to maintain its value.

Yet credible neutrality comes at a cost—literally. Bitcoin consumes significant electricity to sustain proof-of-work. Critics see waste; advocates see a security budget. Banks secure assets with steel vaults, guards, and armed vehicles. Bitcoin secures assets with computational fortresses that cannot be bribed, coerced, or corrupted by insider fraud. Energy expenditure places a real-world price on transaction finality, converting electrons into defence against double-spend attacks and censorship attempts. The controversy is real. It forces a clear reckoning with trade-offs: how much energy should the assurance of incorruptible settlement demand? As energy systems decarbonise and renewable overcapacity grows, Bitcoin mining may support grid stability rather than undermine sustainability. But those scenarios remain contested. The debate itself illuminates the political nature of security.

Throughout this chapter, a quiet motif will reappear: the idea of a ledger that belongs to everyone and no one. In traditional finance, ledgers are private property. Banks and clearinghouses maintain internal records, granting exported trust only to verified participants. Bitcoin flips the arrangement. The ledger is public, auditable by anyone, broadcast to all. Time is measured collectively. Ownership is proven cryptographically. Governance emerges from distributed agreement rather than regulatory decree. The network does not ask who you are. It asks only whether the rules were followed.

The significance of this experiment extends beyond monetary theory. It touches the lived reality of individuals for whom the financial system operates less as a service and more as a barrier. People locked out due to geography, politics, or paperwork now encounter a form of money that requires nothing but connectivity and competence. Activists in authoritarian environments use Bitcoin to preserve funds when bank accounts are frozen. Migrants avoid extractive remittance fees by moving value over a borderless network. Families in inflation-scarred economies store wealth in a currency that resists local mismanagement. These stories are neither universal nor unblemished. Volatility remains harsh. Knowledge gaps persist. But they demonstrate why the question of who controls money is not academic.

Bitcoin also raises philosophical challenges for advanced economies. If money can exist outside state issuance, what becomes of the state's role in stabilising value, allocating credit, and responding to crisis? Can a decentralised system coordinate collective welfare? Or does its neutrality abandon those crushed by misfortune? Enthusiasts emphasise empowerment. Skeptics warn of fragility. Both perspectives hold truths. The promise of rules without rulers cannot erase the need for communities, safety nets, and inclusive participation. Monetary freedom means little if it is accessible only to the technically literate.

Yet even critics recognise that Bitcoin has forced a re-evaluation of financial architecture. Central banks contemplate digital currencies not merely as innovation but as defence. Payment giants integrate crypto rails to meet user demand. Custodians build infrastructure to attract institutional capital. Policy debates begin to include the rights of self-custody, the boundaries of surveillance, and the definitions of finality. A decade ago, these topics were niche. Now they are central. Bitcoin's influence emerges not from dominance but from the alternative it embodies.

This chapter, then, traces how Bitcoin converts abstract ideals into operational mechanics: scarcity enforced by difficulty adjustments, autonomy granted through keys, alignment achieved by incentives, and security purchased with energy. And beneath it all, a cultural shift: the invitation to see money as a commons rather than a concession. A system where the right to transact is not granted by approval but recognised by participation.

The story is not finished. Bitcoin is imperfect, evolving, contested. It faces technical challenges, philosophical disputes, regulatory pressures, and environmental scrutiny. Yet those uncertainties are the signal. A living monetary system is never settled. It must prove its worth continuously—block by block, choice by choice.

The previous chapter showed how institutions shaped money with authority, policy, and emergency power. Now we study a network that proposes to shape money with code, consensus, and unyielding rules. To understand that proposal, we must explore the architecture of digital scarcity, the meaning of property without accounts, the incentives that secure truth, and the costs of neutrality.

Make no mistake: this is a different monetary universe. And it invites us to ask a question that reaches to the foundations of trust: If a ledger can govern itself—programmable, transparent, borderless—what room remains for the old gatekeepers to define the limits of our financial lives?

Digital Scarcity by Design

On 3 January 2009, at approximately 18:15 UTC, a computer in an unknown location generated the first block of the Bitcoin blockchain. Embedded in its data was a line from that day's *Times* newspaper in London: *"Chancellor on brink of second bailout for banks."* The message tied the network's birth to a precise moment in monetary history. At that instant, a ledger with no owner began ticking forward like a clock. Every ten minutes, give or take, a new block would appear, containing transactions validated not by decree but by computation. The result was a breakthrough that had eluded computer scientists for decades: a digital asset that remained scarce without relying on any institution to enforce the limit. Scarcity, once guaranteed by physical constraint, was now engineered.

The paradox is striking. Most digital files multiply effortlessly—copy, paste, distribute at zero cost. Yet Bitcoin's supply will never exceed 21 million. To create a new coin requires energy, equipment, and the solving of a cryptographic puzzle against global competition. Proof-of-work links cost to consensus. It turns a public network of strangers into a mechanism of agreement. The difficulty adjustment ensures that the rhythm remains constant even as more machines join the race. Time, reward, and verification are fused into a single process.

A public clock must be trusted by all. Bitcoin achieves this through decentralised measurement: every node verifies the interval between blocks and adjusts expectations accordingly. When new machines increase hashing power, the network does not accelerate issuance; it tightens the puzzle. When miners depart, the puzzle loosens. The behaviour can be seen on any block explorer: roughly every 2,016 blocks—about two weeks—the difficulty changes. The implication is profound. No small faction can distort time. Security scales automatically. The network's heartbeat refuses to rush.

The analogy to precious metals is deliberate. Historically, mining gold required labour and capital. The supply expanded slowly because extraction was difficult. Proof-of-work replicates that constraint digitally. But the cryptographic version is more transparent. Anyone with a node can verify the total supply and issuance schedule. No emperor can secretly clip coins; no central banker can quietly adjust policy. The issuance curve is a social contract made explicit: halving events roughly every four years reduce the subsidy, stretching scarcity across generations. It is a countdown with consequences.

The first halving occurred on 28 November 2012. The block reward dropped from 50 to 25 bitcoins. Miners watched revenue fall instantly. Yet the network continued without hesitation. This real-world test showed the mechanism's resilience. Miners adjusted, hardware became more efficient, and the system honoured its schedule. The second halving in July 2016 and the third in May 2020 repeated the pattern. With each reduction, Bitcoin reinforced a cultural motif: discipline. The clock keeps time irrespective of sentiment.

A counter-example highlights what Bitcoin rejected. When the Bretton Woods system collapsed in August 1971, the U.S. government severed the dollar's convertibility to gold with little warning. Overnight, scarcity became policy-driven rather than resource-bound. That decision enabled monetary flexibility but also increased reliance on institutional judgement. Reconciliation lies in recognising that Bitcoin is an attempt to separate money from discretion. It replaces trust in rulers with trust in computation.

But Bitcoin's design is not without limitation. Proof-of-work consumes substantial energy. According to the Cambridge Bitcoin Electricity Consumption Index (as of June 2023), the network's annual consumption approximated that of a mid-sized country such as the Netherlands. Critics call this wasteful. The behaviour—warehouses of specialised hardware running continuously—makes the criticism visible. Yet the implication demands scrutiny. The expenditure acts as a security budget: attacking the network requires rival energy and capital on a similar scale. Vaults and armoured trucks have always been costly; Bitcoin allocates defence to computation.

Energy also anchors Bitcoin to the physical world. Blocks represent a record of energy committed to truth. To rewrite history, an attacker must expend more energy than the original timeline consumed. This requirement links economic value with thermodynamic cost in a way no previous digital architecture attempted. The motif of the clock reappears: blocks represent time and effort already spent.

Critics present another challenge: can predictable scarcity coexist with practical money? Bitcoin's supply does not respond to economic conditions. In sharp contrast, during the COVID-19 shock, central banks in March 2020 expanded their balance sheets rapidly to prevent liquidity collapse. They acted like elastic reservoirs. Bitcoin refuses elasticity. The implication cuts both ways. Resilience during crisis requires tools Bitcoin does not possess; yet elastic supply invites uncertainty that Bitcoin seeks to avoid. The tension remains unresolved.

Consensus is where Bitcoin's design most clearly diverges from traditional systems. Centralised ledgers rely on privileged actors to validate truth. Bitcoin distributes that function. Full nodes check each block against rules. Miners propose blocks but cannot dictate their acceptance. The behaviour—nodes rejecting invalid proposals—has been seen repeatedly. In March 2013, a minor software bug created two competing chains. Nodes following the majority rule restored consensus within hours. The network's self-correction was not the result of a committee decision but of rule fidelity. The implication is that governance emerges from participants, not overseers.

The public clock therefore serves as more than chronology. It acts as a scoreboard of collective agreement. A longer chain signifies more cumulative work. This weighting of truth by effort ensures that shortcuts do not prevail. Attempts to rewrite history must start from behind, racing against an opponent that has already advanced. Most give up without trying. The game is rigged in favour of honesty.

One might object: if scarcity can be coded, can it not be copied? Indeed, Bitcoin has countless imitators—forks that duplicated the code. But scarcity cannot be cloned socially. The value of Bitcoin derives not from its algorithm alone but from its network of users who agree on its ledger. When Bitcoin Cash forked in August 2017, the two chains diverged. Both shared history; only one kept the majority of economic support. The behaviour—prices and mining power shifting sharply toward Bitcoin—demonstrated that digital scarcity depends on consensus, not just code. Forks teach the same lesson as mints: legitimacy is a collective judgement, not a technical artefact.

The halving mechanism introduces another quiet implication: Bitcoin becomes harder to subsidise over time. Miners will increasingly rely on transaction fees. The transition raises open questions. Will fees alone be sufficient to maintain security? Will the market value the assurance of irreversible settlement enough to pay the cost? The future is hypothetical, yet the system prepares: difficulty responds continuously to miner participation, and block space remains scarce, forcing markets to prioritise.

We return to the motif: the ticking ledger. Every block is a commitment: energy expended, rules upheld, value preserved. Unlike a centralised system, Bitcoin has no authority capable of freezing the mechanism. Its resilience comes from simplicity. Each ten-minute interval is a tiny referendum affirming that the ledger still matters.

Yet there is a decision ahead. How much should society value a monetary system whose guarantees derive from computation rather than institutions? What trade-offs will be tolerated to preserve a public clock free from political pause buttons?

As the blocks accumulate and the halving calendar advances, Bitcoin maintains its wager: that scarcity enforced by physics may prove more enduring than scarcity enforced by trust. The network keeps time. The question is whether we will continue to wind the clock together—or whether some future crisis will ask us to choose between the certainty of rules and the comfort of human intervention.

Property, Bearer, and Keys

On 13 January 2013, James Howells, an IT worker in Newport, Wales, emptied a drawer of old hard drives into a black bin bag and took them to the municipal landfill. Among them lay a small drive containing the private key to 7,500 bitcoins. At the time, the loss was irritating but manageable. Months later, when Bitcoin's price surged, the mistake became irreversible. Newport City Council declined his repeated requests to excavate the landfill. The drive remains buried, its contents mathematically accessible but physically unrecoverable. A fortune sits under tonnes of waste, neither stolen nor spent, simply orphaned. That stark outcome—the sharp, silent edge of digital bearer property—captures the radical reframing Bitcoin introduced. Ownership becomes a verb. You own only what you can sign.

Howells's story is famous not because it is unique but because it exposes a principle normally hidden behind institutional walls. Traditional finance cushions error. A customer who misplaces a debit card calls a helpline; a bank invalidates the lost credential and issues a replacement. Liability rests with institutions precisely because they maintain accounts and control ledgers. Bitcoin removes that cushion. Keys are final. A mis-typed address means irreversible transfer. A forgotten seed phrase means permanent loss. The behaviour is unforgiving: the network enforces possession without exception. The implication is stark. Sovereignty is powerful, but it is costly.

To understand why Bitcoin insists on this architecture, we must recall what property means when unbundled from custodians. A gold coin is a bearer asset. Whoever holds it exercises control. That simplicity—almost archaic in a world of digital intermediaries—forms the conceptual backdrop. Bitcoin restores bearer logic to the digital realm. The network recognises no person, institution, or court. It recognises only signatures derived from private keys. This removes the distinction between legal ownership and operational control. They collapse into one. It is property in its purest form.

But purity rarely survives contact with everyday life. As early as 2011, the collapse of Tokyo-based exchange Mt. Gox revealed the fragility of users managing keys or trusting poorly run intermediaries. When Mt. Gox suspended withdrawals in February 2014, affecting roughly 850,000 bitcoins, it illustrated a second form of loss: not through misplacement, but through centralisation. The behaviour—customers refreshing dashboards that never updated—demonstrated that if keys are not held by the user, the asset ceases to be bearer property. It becomes a promise, reliant on the solvency and competence of an operator. The implication was widely felt across the sector. Bitcoin's sovereignty model was uncompromising; people's habits were not.

At this junction, custody emerged not as failure but as adaptation. Firms like Coinbase, founded in San Francisco in 2012, offered to manage keys on behalf of users, effectively converting Bitcoin back into something resembling an account. The appeal was obvious: password resets, customer support, insurance policies, and regulatory oversight. The behaviour—millions choosing custodial wallets—measured a simple truth. Not everyone wants to hold the key to their own vault. For many, the risk of irreversible loss outweighed the ideological appeal of absolute control. Custodians filled that gap.

Yet the return to custodial models prompts a deeper question: if many users prefer intermediaries, does Bitcoin's design still matter? The reconciliation lies in recognising that custody is elective, not imposed. Anyone can hold their own keys.

Institutions cannot prevent self-custody without rewriting the network's rules—an unlikely prospect given node consensus. In contrast, the banking system makes self-custody impossible. You cannot store your pounds or dollars in a private vault without converting them into another asset. The motif appears here for the first time: a key. A small object, or a sequence of words, becomes the boundary between autonomy and assistance.

Consider a second checkable example. In 2022, during the Canadian truckers' protest, the government ordered financial institutions to freeze certain bank accounts. Activation of the powers was rapid; access vanished overnight. In response, some attempted to use Bitcoin to bypass restrictions. But those who relied on custodial exchanges found themselves subject to the same constraints. Only those who controlled their own keys could transact independently. The behaviour—wallets receiving funds while exchanges blocked withdrawals—offered a visible lesson. Bitcoin's neutrality applies only to bearer property. Intermediated property carries political exposure.

Still, bearer systems face limitations. They place high cognitive demands on users. A 12- or 24-word seed phrase is brittle. People forget, misstore, or share it inadvertently. Hardware wallets can be lost in house fires or seized at borders. The counter-example strengthens the argument: property without accounts forces us to calibrate responsibility carefully. Solutions emerged accordingly. Multi-signature wallets—popularised by firms like BitGo in 2013—distribute control across multiple keys held by separate parties. No single actor can unilaterally move funds. Businesses adopted this to reduce insider risk; families used it to mitigate accidental loss. The motif reappears: keys, but shared.

This movement shows something broader. Bitcoin did not eliminate trust; it diversified it. Instead of relying solely on institutions, users choose blends of personal custody, collaborative custody, or fully delegated models. Each configuration entails a different liability profile. Measuring these choices reveals a behavioural truth: sovereignty is not binary. It exists on a spectrum.

Traditional systems define ownership through identity. Banks verify your passport, your address, your salary history. Bitcoin defines ownership through capability. Can you produce the correct signature? Everything else is irrelevant. This capability-driven model reframes liability in stark terms. If a malicious actor gains access to your private key, the network treats their signature as yours. There is no fraud desk, no reversible entry. The ledger records only valid cryptographic proofs. The implication is unsettling but precise. With full control comes full exposure.

Yet this rigidity also produces resilience. A state cannot freeze Bitcoin by altering an account ledger, because there are no accounts to alter. It would need to seize keys physically or compel custodians. The network's neutrality is mechanical. It does not bend under pressure. For individuals facing capital controls or politically motivated banking blocks, this rigidity is not a flaw but a lifeline.

Still, a question lingers in the background: can a system built around strict property work at global scale without reintroducing central points of weakness? Exchanges remain attractive targets for hacks and regulatory capture. In 2016, Hong Kong–based Bitfinex suffered a breach of 119,756 bitcoins despite using a multi-signature scheme. The behaviour—attackers exploiting software integration rather than cryptography—exposed the systemic risk of large custodians. Concentration creates honeypots. Users pay for convenience with exposure. The implication is familiar from earlier chapters: infrastructure shapes outcomes more than ideals.

The motif of the key returns again. It invites a simple question: who should hold it? The answer varies across contexts. High-net-worth individuals may choose hardware devices and geographic redundancy. Retail users may opt for custodial platforms subject to local regulation. Activists may rely on seed phrases memorised, risking personal burden for political freedom. Corporations may require audited multi-signature controls. Bitcoin accommodates these choices without demanding uniformity. It presents a foundational layer of bearer property upon which varied custody practices can be built.

A deeper philosophical shift emerges when ownership no longer depends on recognition by an authority. Property becomes portable, borderless, and resistant to censorship. Yet the same structure that empowers dissidents challenges legal systems that adjudicate inheritance, fraud, or disputes. If an heir lacks a seed phrase, the estate cannot recover funds. Courts can assign rights but cannot enforce transfers without cooperation from key holders. The limitation is concrete. Legal frameworks adapt slowly to assets that ignore their jurisdictional boundaries. The reconciliation appears in experiments with social recovery and hybrid models where notaries, lawyers, or fiduciaries hold fragments of control. These innovations aim to marry sovereignty with support.

Metrics reveal the shape of this shift. Chainalysis (2022) estimated that roughly 3.7 million bitcoins may be lost permanently, much of it from early years when users misunderstood the stakes. The behaviour—millions of coins unmoved for over a decade—quantifies the cost of untempered autonomy. Yet these losses also show an inverse truth: coins that survive years of key custody reinforce the legitimacy of bearer ownership. They demonstrate that the system does not degrade without supervision. Property endures through time.

Bitcoin's architecture, then, reframes the core question: what does it mean to own something? Not to rent access, not to rely on institutional endorsement, but to command it directly through cryptographic authority. That autonomy brings sharp trade-offs. Those trade-offs reshape not only finance but also the moral expectations around responsibility, resilience, and error.

As more people engage with Bitcoin—whether directly or through intermediaries—the lines between sovereignty and support will be tested. Custody models will evolve. Regulators will seek clarity. Users will confront the tension between convenience and control. The key motif lingers in the background like a quiet challenge.

At the next turning point, when a user must choose where to store their value, the question will hover: Do you trust your memory, your devices, your chosen custodians—or the network's uncompromising logic of possession?

Incentives and Game Theory

At 20:16 UTC on 1 August 2017, a group of miners in Shenzhen pointed their machines to a new chain and began producing blocks under altered rules. The event created Bitcoin Cash, a fork of the Bitcoin network born from a dispute over block size. Within hours, exchanges from Hong Kong to London listed the new asset, and hash power visibly oscillated as miners chased whichever chain offered the higher immediate return. Watching the diverging ledgers in real time made one fact unmistakable: Bitcoin's stability is not granted; it is chosen. Its rules hold because those who secure the network believe the dominant chain is worth more than its alternatives. The moment that belief shifts, incentives redraw the map. This is how governance functions in a stateless system: not through edict, but through coordination.

The Shenzhen fork crystallised a paradox familiar to economists but rarely so exposed to public view. The cost of securing Bitcoin had, by that point, surpassed millions of dollars per day, yet the network relied on voluntary alignment rather than hierarchical command. The logic was visible in miner dashboards showing fluctuating block rewards; in node logs rejecting blocks that violated the consensus rules; in user behaviour as traders assigned market prices to each chain. At the centre sat a question that animates this subchapter: how do self-interested actors produce a reliable monetary system without a central authority? The short answer is incentives. The long answer is a dynamic interplay of rewards, rules, threats, and expectations—an interplay that invites deeper scrutiny.

Bitcoin's architecture distributes power across three constituencies. Miners assemble blocks and expend energy to secure the chain. Nodes validate transactions and enforce the consensus rules. Users anchor value by choosing which version of the ledger they recognise. These groups act according to measurable incentives: miners pursue revenue, nodes uphold software-defined constraints, users chase liquidity and stability. Their coordination resembles a strategic equilibrium. Not perfect. Not guaranteed. But resilient.

To see how each group shapes the others, return briefly to the 2017 fork. When Bitcoin Cash launched, miners could earn higher short-term profits mining its lower-difficulty chain. But many returned to Bitcoin within days. Why? Because users, who ultimately decide which asset holds value, remained with the original chain. The behaviour—exchanges reporting deep liquidity for BTC and thinner order books for BCH—signalled where long-term rewards lay. The implication is clear. In Bitcoin's governance, miners follow users, not the reverse. Hash power moves where value flows.

Name this mechanism: credible neutrality. It describes how the dominant chain earns loyalty not by favouring particular groups but by minimising special treatment. Neutral rules attract broad support because they reduce the risk of capture. When the rules apply equally to all, no actor expects favourable exceptions. This neutrality is why full nodes reject blocks that break the protocol's fundamental limits, regardless of who mined them. The behaviour is mechanical, not political. A block exceeding the weight limit is invalidated instantly, even if a powerful mining pool produced it. The implication is profound. Authority sits not with miners, but with the collective enforcement of rules by those running independent software.

Yet neutrality does not remove conflict. It channels it. Disputes in Bitcoin manifest as forks—economic tests of preference. This is not a sign of failure; it is the system's safety valve. When consensus fractures, participants reveal their priorities through action: pointing hash rate, running particular node software, or pricing assets differently. A fork is a public reckoning. It shows who is willing to bear cost to uphold a principle, whether that principle is transactional throughput, immutability, or decentralisation.

Consider a second example: the activation of Segregated Witness (SegWit) in 2017. The proposal had broad support among developers and users but faced resistance from influential miners. As tensions rose, a group of companies and miners meeting in New York in May 2017 announced the "New York Agreement," aiming to bundle SegWit activation with a subsequent block size increase. But users, represented by thousands of node operators worldwide, prepared a counter-move: a User Activated Soft Fork (UASF), scheduled for 1 August 2017. The UASF set a simple condition. After a specified date, nodes would accept only blocks signalling SegWit support. Miners who refused to adopt the upgrade risked mining blocks the majority of the network would reject.

This was a game-theoretic gambit. It exploited the asymmetry between miners' short-term incentives—to avoid operational risk—and their long-term need for users' trust. When 1 August arrived, miners overwhelmingly signalled support for SegWit. The behaviour was decisive. Faced with the prospect of mining worthless blocks, miners aligned with node operators. The implication was unmistakable: users, not miners, anchor Bitcoin's governance. They can impose constraints by collectively enforcing software rules.

But every rule-driven system faces a counter-example. What if a powerful coalition of miners, exchanges, and custodians attempted to push through a change that users disliked? Could they overwhelm the network's neutrality? In theory, such a coalition could create social pressure, market liquidity, and hash power to promote a contentious fork. The limitation is real. Influence clusters around large intermediaries. Yet the reconciliation lies in the cost structure. To override users' choice, the coalition would need to convince them to move their economic weight to the new chain. Without that migration, the fork would produce a chain with security but no value. The economic majority, not the computational majority, determines survival. This is why tiny nodes run by ordinary users still matter. They enforce constraints that miners ignore at their peril.

A quiet motif threads through these dynamics: commitment. Miners commit energy. Nodes commit validation. Users commit economic weight. These commitments are public and observable. They shape expectations, and expectations shape outcomes. In Bitcoin, coordination emerges not from shared identity or allegiance but from converging incentives visible in each participant's behaviour.

Metrics illuminate this. As of March 2023, Bitcoin's global hash rate surpassed 350 exahashes per second (source: Hashrate Index, 2023). This immense expenditure expresses miners' belief that their investment will be rewarded. Similarly, over

15,000 reachable nodes (Bitcoin Core stats, 2023) enforce the consensus rules. These independent validators reflect a decentralised commitment to neutrality. Meanwhile, markets price Bitcoin at scales that reflect users' collective assessment of its stability relative to alternatives. These numbers are not abstractions. They are votes cast in computation, verification, and liquidity.

Game theory helps explain why this equilibrium holds. In repeated games, cooperation emerges when defection carries long-term cost. A miner tempted to cheat—by inserting invalid transactions or attempting a double spend—faces immediate penalties. The network discards non-conforming blocks. Honest miners continue building atop the legitimate chain, leaving the cheater with unrecoverable losses. The expected behaviour discourages deviation. The implication: Bitcoin's rules align self-interest with network health.

Still, the incentives are not static. The block subsidy halves every four years. As rewards fall, transaction fees must eventually sustain miners. This introduces tension. If fees spike unpredictably, users may seek alternative systems. If fees remain low, miners may underinvest in security. The motif of commitment reappears. What level of commitment from users—via fees—is necessary to support miner commitment to hash rate? This is not a settled question. It is a scenario the network will navigate over decades.

A third example shows the stakes. During the mempool congestion of May 2023, average transaction fees temporarily exceeded US$30 (Blockchain.com data, May 2023). Users delayed non-urgent transactions or relied on batching. Miners enjoyed an unexpected windfall. Critics argued that high fees threatened Bitcoin's utility for everyday payments. Supporters countered that fee-driven security strengthens long-term resilience. Both behaviours reveal something essential: equilibrium depends on adaptive expectations. If users accept occasional fee spikes as part of securing a scarce settlement layer, they maintain commitment. If not, they may drift to competing systems. Incentives do not dictate outcomes. They shape probabilities.

Credible neutrality ties these threads together. Because Bitcoin treats all valid transactions equally, regardless of sender, amount, or purpose, users trust the system to remain unbiased. This trust is not sentimental. It is rooted in observed behaviour: nodes rejecting invalid blocks consistently; miners treated as interchangeable; no institution wielding discretionary power over the ledger. The implication is practical. Neutrality lowers coordination costs. When rules are predictable, actors can commit without fear of arbitrary change.

Yet neutrality must be defended. Centralisation—whether of mining pools, node hosting, or exchange infrastructure—threatens the credibility of rule enforcement. A highly concentrated mining industry could, in theory, censor transactions or delay block propagation. The counter-example is visible in episodes where mining pools briefly exceeded 51 percent of hash rate, such as GHash.io in 2014. The community responded with social pressure and voluntary hash rate redistribution. The reconciliation is not guaranteed, but it is observable. Actors chose to preserve neutrality. Incentives aligned with stability.

The final tension sits quietly beneath all of this. Bitcoin relies on rational actors who prefer long-term network health over short-term unilateral gain. But rationality is contextual. It depends on political pressures, market volatility, regulatory signals, and human error. The game is repeated, but the players change. New miners enter. Old users leave. Nodes upgrade. Exchanges evolve. Incentives shift with each external shock.

When the next contentious proposal arises—whether about fees, privacy, or block structure—the strategic question will return: do the incentives of miners, nodes, and users still converge strongly enough to maintain credible neutrality? The answer will not come from promises. It will emerge from action. The commitments each group chooses to make will script the next chapter of Bitcoin's governance.

Energy, Security, and Externalities

At 03:14 on 20 July 2021, the operators of Iceland's Landsvirkjun power stations watched their load dashboards flicker. A cluster of industrial customers—mostly data centres near Keflavík—had collectively drawn more than 100 megawatts within minutes. One site, run by Genesis Mining, had just activated a tranche of machines redirected from China after the June 2021 crackdown. The demand spike was not an accident. It reflected a migration of computational security: miners seeking low-cost, renewable energy to anchor Bitcoin's proof-of-work. By sunrise, the new load had stabilised, Iceland's grid had absorbed the surge, and global hash rate charts showed a visible uptick. The episode distilled a question that would animate policy circles for months: when energy use expresses a security budget, how do we measure its worth?

The paradox seemed sharp. At a moment when European governments debated energy rationing, a decentralised network had redirected equipment across continents to restore the integrity of its ledger. Critics invoked carbon metrics; supporters pointed to grid curtailment data and renewable penetration rates. The tension played out in numbers and behaviours, not slogans. The spike in Iceland followed an observable pattern: miners move where energy is cheapest, stranded, or curtailed. Their presence forces a reckoning. Energy consumption is not incidental to Bitcoin; it is fundamental. It buys honesty.

The idea that security carries a measurable cost is not new. The Bank of England's vault under Threadneedle Street, reinforced in 1939 after concerns about wartime bombing, required steel thicknesses specified in tonnes and construction budgets recorded in archived ledgers. Gold bars stacked behind those walls represented concentrated energy expenditure from mining companies in South Africa, Australia, and Canada. Physical security relied on mass, space, and guards. Bitcoin's security relies on computation, electricity, and broad participation. The shift from vault to algorithm marks a change in architectural logic, not in purpose.

Show this by naming behaviours. In 2022, Texas grid operator ERCOT published data noting that flexible mining loads could curtail during peak demand by over 1 gigawatt (ERCOT, 2022). The behaviour was visible: miners switched off rigs during heat waves, freeing capacity. Then, during surplus hours, they resumed operations, absorbing excess wind and solar output that would otherwise have been curtailed. The implication is structural. Bitcoin mining behaves like a dispatchable data load, responsive to price signals.

But the counter-example is equally real. In Kazakhstan in early 2022, unregulated mining clusters contributed to grid strain, prompting nationwide power cuts and prompting authorities to disconnect illicit farms. Here, mining did not behave as a stabiliser. It behaved as an unmeasured stressor. The limitation matters. It shows that mining is not inherently beneficial or harmful. Its impact depends on governance, grid conditions, and the incentives facing operators. Reconciling the cases demands precision. Where grids have transparency, pricing, and spare capacity, mining acts as a flexible load. Where governance is weak, it can exacerbate fragility.

A quiet motif emerges: fortresses. Old ones and new. The physical fortress of gold requires walls and guards. The computational fortress of Bitcoin requires energy and decentralised miners. The question is not whether fortresses cost resources; it is what security model they sustain, and at what external cost.

To compare vaults and mining farms, trace the energy expenditure chain. Gold mining requires explosives, earth moving, chemical processing, and global transport. According to the World Gold Council (2021), the average energy intensity of gold extraction and refining totals tens of millions of gigajoules annually, varying by ore grade. The activity concentrates environmental impact in specific regions. Its security value comes from physical scarcity: bars locked in vaults.

Bitcoin's expenditure, by contrast, is location-agnostic. Cambridge University's Centre for Alternative Finance estimated Bitcoin's energy use at around 100–150 TWh per year in 2022. The footprint shifts with geography. Hydropower in Sichuan during the rainy season, geothermal in Iceland, wind in Texas, stranded gas in North Dakota flares converted into electricity. The behaviour is mobile. This mobility tightens the link between energy markets and security budgets.

Expenditure signals commitment. A miner who deploys capital to acquire hardware and power expresses belief in the network's long-term value. The network, in turn, rewards honest behaviour by recognising valid blocks. The mechanism resembles a repeated auction where the price of honesty is measured in kilowatt-hours. This ties the abstraction of "security" to a metric: hash rate. A higher hash rate makes attacks costlier. As of March 2023, global hash rate exceeded 350 exahashes per second (Hashrate Index, 2023), reflecting billions invested in physical infrastructure.

Yet energy use alone does not buy legitimacy. It must be contextualised. A vault with walls three metres thick is secure but useless if the currency it defends lacks public confidence. Bitcoin mining burns electricity, but its output—a ledger settled every ten minutes—matters only if users value immutability. Security budgets, whether physical or computational, are justified only when they guard assets considered foundational. This is why debates over Bitcoin's energy use grow sharper as adoption widens. The larger the economic weight anchored to the chain, the stronger the case for a robust security budget.

Still, externalities demand scrutiny. CO_2 emissions vary dramatically by energy source. A study by Krause and Tolaymat (2018) estimated that in 2017 Bitcoin's carbon intensity mirrored that of average global electricity grids. But by 2022, with mining shifting towards regions rich in renewables and curtailed energy, estimates had begun to diverge. The Bitcoin Mining Council, an industry group, claimed in 2022 that over 58 percent of mining used sustainable sources. Critics challenged the methodology. The tension reveals the difficulty of verification. Unlike the Bank of England's vault—whose steel and stone are fixed—mining infrastructure evolves rapidly. Measuring externalities requires continuous data, not static assumptions.

Consider a second example. In Norway, where hydropower dominates electricity generation, mining firms such as Kryptovault established operations in 2018, taking advantage of low-cost renewable energy near Hønefoss. Local authorities raised concerns about noise and heat, prompting regulatory reviews. Yet the carbon footprint was negligible due to near-zero-emission electricity. The behaviour shows that externalities are multi-dimensional. Carbon is only one dimension; community impact is another. The implication is that sustainable mining requires more than green electricity. It requires social licence and adaptive infrastructure management.

Then take the counter-example of fossil-heavy grids. In regions where coal dominates, such as parts of Inner Mongolia before China's 2021 mining ban, Bitcoin mining amplified carbon emissions. The behaviour prompted policy intervention. China's National Development and Reform Commission cited energy inefficiency and environmental concerns when ordering shutdowns. How do we reconcile these cases? By recognising that externalities are contingent. Mining amplifies the characteristics of the grid it inhabits. A clean grid produces clean security. A dirty grid produces dirty security.

The quiet motif of fortresses returns. A fortress is judged not only by its walls but by what it demands of its surroundings. A vault consumes land and steel. A data centre consumes electricity and generates heat. Neither is neutral. Both reshape their context.

Cleaner-grid pathways offer a route to align Bitcoin's security budget with broader energy transitions. These pathways are not predictions; they are scenarios grounded in existing behaviour. One scenario involves miners colocating with renewable generators to absorb intermittent supply, smoothing revenue for wind and solar farms. ERCOT's curtailment data illustrates this potential. Another scenario involves flare gas mitigation. Companies like Crusoe Energy, active in Colorado and North Dakota since 2018, deploy systems that capture methane from oilfields, converting it into electricity used for mining. Methane has far higher warming potential than CO_2. Burning it for electricity reduces emissions relative to venting. The behaviour aligns incentives: oil producers reduce liability, miners secure low-cost power, and emissions fall.

A third scenario involves demand response. As grids incorporate more renewables, volatility increases. Mining loads, with near-instant ramp-down capacity, can stabilise frequency and offer ancillary services. In December 2022, Texas miners curtailed significant load during cold snaps, contributing to grid stability. These are not abstract claims. They are documented actions with measurable outcomes.

Yet these pathways have limits. They rely on regulatory frameworks, public trust, and transparent reporting. Without these, mining risks entrenching poor energy practices. A fortress built on unstable ground becomes a liability. The question becomes whether mining can commit credibly to beneficial behaviours. Commitment requires visibility, which in turn requires data. Independent audits of energy sources, carbon accounting aligned with internationally recognised standards, and transparent reporting from mining pools would improve credibility. The implication is that governance—soft and hard—shapes the externalities of computational fortresses.

Returning to the motif, fortresses evolve. The Bank of England expanded its vaults during the Second World War because threats changed. Bitcoin miners relocate across continents because energy markets and regulations shift. Both systems adapt by reallocating resources. Both express security budgets in tangible form. But only one can align itself fluidly with cleaner energy if incentives point in that direction.

The unresolved tension rests with a simple question. As Bitcoin's block subsidy declines and fees must increasingly sustain miners, what mix of energy sources will operators commit to? The answer will not appear in declarations. It will appear in where machines hum, which grids they inhabit, and what externalities they absorb or mitigate. The next phase of Bitcoin's security budget will be written not only in exahashes but in kilowatt-hours, emissions audits, and public trust.

Chapter 3
How Banks Make Money From Money

Before sunrise, on an ordinary weekday, the financial system begins its quiet choreography. Somewhere in Manchester, a young couple wakes to an alert from their bank: their pay has cleared. The numbers on their screen rise, a digital reassurance that another month's labour has translated into purchasing power. At that exact moment, far from their thoughts, that same deposit is already in motion. It is being counted, aggregated, and set to work—financing a loan for someone they have never met, perhaps the warehouse expansion of a firm they will never visit. The promise implicit in the numbers—the right to spend whenever they choose—rests on a delicate truth: most of that money has already left the building.

This silent mobilisation of deposits is the first sleight of modern banking. The couple believes their funds are safe, available on demand. The bank must ensure they are—yet it simultaneously lends those funds out for years. Borrowing short, lending long. The system's magic lies in turning individual trust into collective credit. But magic, as any illusionist knows, relies on precise timing, flawless stagecraft, and an audience that wants to believe. Remove confidence, and the show collapses.

All banking begins with a promise. The deposits we hold are liabilities of institutions that owe us redemption on demand. Mortgages, business loans, and government bonds, meanwhile, are assets that pay back slowly. In between lies maturity transformation—the art of earning interest on long-term lending while keeping short-term claimants content. It is profitable. It is productive. It is inherently fragile. For centuries, this fragility was contained by gold reserves, then by increasingly complex regulatory structures, and today by the assumption that central banks will intervene if belief falters.

Every financial crisis replays the same drama in different costumes. A queue forms outside a branch. Headlines scream "liquidity crunch." Behind the scenes, repayment schedules and collateral constraints tighten like a vise. The numbers that once felt solid reveal their contingency. Banking is revealed for what it is: confidence staged as accounting. Haircuts on collateral, capital ratios debated in regulatory filings, the murmur of repo markets opening just before dawn—all are techniques to sustain this confidence. When they work, risk feels invisible. When they fail, risk becomes the headline.

Yet banks do more than mediate credit. They sit at the core of the payments system—the railways of money in this chapter's earlier terms. Every tap of a card, every payroll run, every recurring subscription routes through their infrastructure. They charge for these passages in ways that seldom draw attention: a few basis points on interchange here, a maintenance fee there, the quiet profit of float—the earnings from balances held in transit. They also harvest something new: data. Who buys what, when, and where is commercial intelligence. By shaping behaviour—steering us toward preferred merchants, locking us in with convenience—they monetise not only the movement of money but the story it tells about our lives.

Scale deepens this influence. A small bank must obey the system. A colossal one can shape it. "Too big to fail" is sometimes framed as a rescue policy; more accurately, it is a recognition of dependence. When an institution becomes so interwoven with payments, savings, and credit allocation that its failure would destabilise the state, it gains leverage. Bargaining power grows in the shadows: regulatory exceptions, policy influence, implicit guarantees. Banks that reach this scale do not merely participate in markets—they define them.

This chapter invites the reader to watch the machinery rather than the display. The familiar symbols—ATMs, account balances, clever marketing that dresses finance in friendliness—can obscure what lies beneath: an intricate set of incentives, privileges, and political bargains. The business of money is not passive administration; it is active creation. When a loan is made, new purchasing power enters the economy. When a credit line is reduced, purchasing power disappears. Banks profit from this creation, yet society bears the consequences when it misfires.

The tension is not moral but structural. Banks must pursue profits for shareholders. They must also preserve confidence for the public. At times, these missions align beautifully: lending supports growth, payments speed commerce, risk techniques contain shocks. At other times, they conflict: margins tempt overreach, opacity protects rents, and stability hinges on public backstops extended without public consent. The industry's success depends on never running out of trust, even as it monetises that trust daily.

As new technologies and decentralised alternatives challenge incumbents, banks face a choice. They can reshape their models, embracing transparency and shared rails—or they can double down on their central role, leaning on systemic importance as both shield and sword. The stakes reach beyond balance sheets. They define who allocates capital, who controls data, and who absorbs losses when growth sours.

Money circulates. Influence concentrates. Those who manage the circulation accumulate power that shapes economies and, by extension, politics. The infrastructure beneath our everyday transactions is not neutral. It privileges certain actors and constraints others. To understand modern finance, we must ask not only how money moves, but who earns from its movement—and on what terms.

This chapter turns the lights up on the stage. It follows the flow of deposits into mortgages and securities, revealing where profit lives within the pipeline. It examines risk not as a spreadsheet abstraction but as a choreography requiring constant motion. It shows how payments architecture extracts value from every act of exchange. And it confronts the logic of bigness—the point at which scale becomes sovereignty-lite.

The questions are uncomfortable, but essential. What do we owe institutions that promise stability yet require rescue? Should profits be private while losses remain socialised? How much opacity is too much? And if banks hold the power to make money from money, who holds the power to judge when that power has gone too far?

The pages ahead will not provide ideology dressed as insight. They will describe the system as it operates: ingenious, indispensable, and periodically dangerous. A system that has funded growth, expanded opportunity, and also, at times, tested the limits of public patience. A system that remains the dominant interface between people and their economic lives.

We return, then, to that young couple in Manchester. Their payslip arrived, their balance rose, and their bank made money—from their money. As long as they trust that the numbers will be there tomorrow, the system hums. The moment doubt enters the equation, everything changes. The foundation of modern finance is neither metal nor code. It is belief.

Understanding how that belief is earned, priced, and occasionally broken is the work of this chapter. And the questions it opens are not academic. They concern every card we tap, every loan we take, every deposit we trust to remain whole.

Maturity Transformation 101

On 10 March 2023, regulators closed Silicon Valley Bank in Santa Clara, California, after depositors tried to pull tens of billions of dollars in two days. The bank had not failed because its loans had suddenly soured or its staff had vanished. It failed because of time. Short-term deposits, which customers assumed could be withdrawn at will, had been parked in longer-term securities that would only pay out fully years in the future. When depositors demanded their money *now*, the bank could deliver only *later*. The gap between those words was fatal.

This was not an exotic fintech experiment gone wrong; it was banking in its purest form. Silicon Valley Bank had done what banks are built to do: transform a stream of unstable, on-demand funding into long-term credit for mortgages, startups, and Treasury securities. It had built a bridge between savers who wanted instant access and borrowers who needed years to repay. The bridge begins with deposits. It ends, if all goes well, with houses, factories, and companies that did not exist before the loan. The margin in between—the difference between what the bank pays its depositors and what it charges its borrowers—is where profit lives. It is also where fragility hides.

At the heart of this process is a simple but unsettling fact: if every depositor turned up at once, virtually no bank could pay them all. Your savings account is not a labelled box in a vault. It is part of a pool of funding, constantly reallocated. In normal times, this does not matter. Few people demand all their cash at once. Banks rely on patterns: salaries coming in, bills going out, balances fluctuating within a band. The mathematics of those flows underpins their business. They know, statistically, how many people are likely to withdraw today, this week, this month. They do *not* expect everyone.

Maturity transformation is the name we give to that decision to borrow short and lend long. Show it through the most mundane of transactions. You deposit your wages at a branch in Leeds. The bank credits your account and, in its internal systems, books an inexpensive liability: it owes you money that you can reclaim on demand. Somewhere else, across the country, a family in Bristol applies for a twenty-five-year mortgage. The bank approves. The funds the couple in Leeds will not touch for years—because in practice they keep a fairly stable buffer—become part of the mortgage pipeline. On one side, a sight deposit paying minimal interest. On the other, a long-term loan at a higher rate. The spread between the two pays salaries, absorbs losses, and provides returns to shareholders.

Name this pipeline for what it is: a time machine for capital. It pulls future repayment streams into the present so projects can begin. It allows a builder to lay bricks today based on income that will only arrive over decades of mortgage payments. Without it, home ownership rates would fall, businesses would struggle to expand, and governments would find infrastructure financing far more difficult. The implication is clear. Society has chosen to tolerate maturity mismatch because it accelerates growth. We live in houses and work in offices that exist only because banks promised the future to the present.

But the same mechanism can reverse at speed. When the couple in Leeds hears worrying news—perhaps a rumour on social media that their bank is "in trouble"—their behaviour changes. They pull funds into a supposedly safer institution or into a money market fund. Their friends do the same. What was once a stable deposit base becomes a stampede. The bank's balance sheet has not changed overnight; its assets are still long-term loans and securities. Yet its liabilities have become impatient. The bridge of time is suddenly demanded back, plank by plank, right now.

That is why liquidity buffers exist. Regulators require banks to hold stocks of assets that can be sold quickly without huge losses—central bank reserves, government bonds, high-quality securities. These buffers are meant to buy time: time to sell assets gradually rather than at fire-sale prices; time to access central bank facilities; time to reassure markets. The Liquidity Coverage Ratio in frameworks like Basel III essentially measures whether a bank can withstand a short, sharp outflow of funding. Behind the acronym lies a human scene: will the bank have enough readily usable money if depositors queue at cashpoints and flood online banking portals tomorrow morning?

Look at Northern Rock in September 2007 to see what happens when the answer is "no." The British mortgage lender had funded itself heavily through short-term wholesale markets rather than sticky retail deposits. When those markets froze, its liquidity buffer proved inadequate. The images of savers queuing outside branches in Newcastle were the visible manifestation of an invisible mismatch: a book of long-dated mortgages financed by fragile, flighty funding. The Bank of England's emergency support could not prevent reputational damage; the firm was nationalised. The implication is sobering. A bank can be solvent in an accounting sense—its assets exceed its liabilities—and still fail because it cannot pay quickly enough.

Where maturity transformation succeeds, it does so by respecting three constraints. First, diversification of funding: not relying excessively on any one source of short-term money. Secondly, careful measurement of duration gaps: aligning the average life of assets with the stability of liabilities. Thirdly, realistic assumptions about depositor behaviour in stress. The last is the hardest. Modelling "normal" drawdowns is one thing; modelling viral panic in a group chat is another. The shift from people visiting branches to moving millions with a smartphone has compressed the time window within which banks must respond. The run can happen before the queue is visible.

A counter-example helps clarify the structure by showing its absence. Narrow banks—institutions that hold 100 per cent reserves against deposits and do not lend long—avoid maturity transformation. Historical proposals like the Chicago Plan in the 1930s, and more recently Switzerland's Vollgeld initiative, have argued for such full-reserve models. In theory, a narrow bank cannot suffer a run in the same way; every pound deposited is matched by a pound in safe assets. But the limitation becomes evident elsewhere. Credit creation must then migrate to entities that *do* take maturity risk—shadow banks, capital markets, non-bank lenders. The bridge of time does not disappear. It simply moves off the high street and into less visible institutions.

Reconciling these perspectives reveals that maturity transformation is not optional in a credit economy; it is a question of where, by whom, and under what rules. We can insist that only tightly regulated banks perform it, with explicit backstops from central banks. Or we can allow it to proliferate outside the regulatory perimeter, where opacity is greater. We cannot wish it away. The desire of savers to keep funds liquid and the desire of borrowers to commit for the long term will always require a bridge.

Within banks, that bridge is managed day by day by treasury desks that few customers ever think about. These teams monitor cash positions, forecast inflows and outflows, decide when to issue longer-term debt, and when to draw on central bank lines. They live in spreadsheets of mismatches: assets maturing in one month versus liabilities repricing in one week; securities that can be repo'd overnight; contingencies for stressed scenarios. Their decisions express the institution's risk tolerance. A treasury that stretches too far—maximising margin by locking funds into longer-term assets—

earns extra profit *until* markets move. Then it discovers how quickly a comfortable cushion becomes a cliff-edge.

Central banks hover behind this architecture as lenders of last resort. When depositors and markets flee simultaneously, private liquidity buffers prove insufficient. A central bank can extend collateralised loans against long-term assets, effectively swapping illiquid securities for cash. This role is codified in standing facilities and emergency programmes. During the 2008 crisis and the 2020 pandemic, such interventions prevented wholesale funding freezes from turning into systemic collapse. The behaviour—banks pledging mortgages and securities in exchange for central bank reserves—makes maturity transformation sustainable at scale. The implication, however, is political. The state underwrites the bridge.

Once the state stands behind banks, the question of margins becomes a public one. How much profit is reasonable for institutions whose business model depends on publicly guaranteed deposits and central bank backstops? When interest rates rise quickly, banks may widen the gap between what they earn on loans and what they pay on deposits, especially if customers are slow to move into higher-yielding products. The spread, widened by inertia, becomes a transfer from inattentive savers to bank shareholders. It is not illegal; it is the system functioning as designed. But it forces a normative question: how should we evaluate the fairness of profits earned on the back of maturity transformation?

The quiet motif here is time. Time as opportunity. Time as risk. Time as a contested resource. Savers want the option value of instant access; borrowers want the security of fixed repayment schedules; banks sit between them, slicing and recombining time horizons into portfolios. When trust in this time-slicing is high, the system appears almost frictionless. Direct debits clear, mortgages renew, overdrafts cover gaps. When trust evaporates, time contracts brutally. Everyone wants their money *today*, no one is willing to commit to *tomorrow*, and the bridge collapses.

That collapse does not always look like a queue outside a branch. It can be subtler: a tightening of lending standards; a refusal to roll over short-term corporate funding; a rise in mortgage rates that prices out new buyers. These are all ways in which banks shorten the terms at which they are willing to lend when they fear their own funding may not last. The effect ripples outward. Investment projects are delayed, hiring slows, and growth falters. Time, withdrawn from the system, takes potential with it.

As debates over digital currencies, narrow banking, and decentralised finance intensify, maturity transformation will sit at the centre of the argument. Some will argue that technology can reduce the need for intermediaries to bear time risk. Others will insist that only institutions with balance sheets and regulators can safely perform this function. Both camps must answer the same question.

How much mismatch between "you can have your money now" and "we will get our money back later" is acceptable for a society that depends on credit to build its future?

Risk, Collateral, and Confidence

On the morning of 15 September 2008, in midtown Manhattan, a small army of lawyers and traders filed into the offices of the Federal Reserve Bank of New York. Lehman Brothers had filed for bankruptcy that day. On the whiteboards, staff sketched sprawling maps of repo trades, collateral chains, and counterparty exposures. Overnight loans backed by supposedly safe securities had evaporated. The haircuts on collateral—tiny percentages shaved off value to cover risk—suddenly ballooned. Positions that had looked sound on Friday were unsustainable by Monday. What changed? Not the ink on the contracts, not the coupons on the bonds, but one intangible variable: confidence. The moment markets stopped believing, the numbers in the ledgers meant something else.

Banking is often described as "managing risk". That sounds clinical, almost neutral. What Lehman revealed—what every crisis reveals—is that banking is confidence staged as accounting. The ledgers give that confidence a language: risk-weighted assets, Tier 1 capital ratios, liquidity coverage metrics. Haircuts in repo markets measure how much doubt lenders have about the collateral they accept. Capital buffers measure how much loss a bank can absorb before its liabilities exceed its assets. As long as confidence holds, these numbers reassure. When confidence breaks, they become contested, revised, reinterpreted in real time.

Begin with collateral, because it is the most tactile expression of trust. When two institutions enter a repurchase agreement—a repo—the borrower hands over securities as collateral and receives cash. The lender applies a haircut: if the bond is worth £100, they might lend £98. The £2 gap is a cushion against price moves. For a gilt issued by the UK government, that haircut might be tiny. For a mortgage-backed security linked to subprime borrowers in Florida, the haircut might be far larger. The size is not arbitrary; it encodes a judgement about risk. When markets are calm, haircuts compress. Lenders compete. When stress rises, haircuts widen brutally. Balance sheets that assumed low haircuts discover they were borrowing more belief than cash.

The US tri-party repo market in 2007–2008 is a textbook example. For years, securities of all kinds—Treasuries, corporate bonds, structured products—flowed through it each night as dealers funded their inventories. Salomon Brothers in the 1990s, then Bear Stearns and Lehman, made this overnight market the central vein of their funding. As mortgage securities began to wobble, lenders raised haircuts on those assets. At first by a sliver, then by double digits. What had been near-cash became hard to fund. The implication was viciously simple: when collateral is downgraded by sentiment, funding disappears. Institutions that look solvent on paper find themselves unable to roll overnight repo.

A quieter episode in Europe shows the same mechanics. During the eurozone sovereign debt crisis, Greek government bonds once treated as risk-free began to attract punitive haircuts in European repo markets. Banks that had pledged them found they could borrow less against the same nominal amount. They needed to find more collateral or accept shrinking balance sheets. The European Central Bank intervened, accepting stressed sovereign bonds in its own facilities to ease the squeeze. Behaviour again revealed the point: official support can partially substitute for lost market confidence, but only for those inside the club.

The motif of the haircut runs through these stories. It is a small accounting adjustment with large consequences. Who decides how much to shave off, and when, shapes the availability of credit far beyond individual trades. Haircuts tighten, credit shrinks.

Capital ratios tell a parallel story, but on a slower timescale. They measure how much loss-absorbing equity a bank holds relative to its risk-weighted assets. The Basel Accords, negotiated first in 1988 and revised after 2008, codified minimum capital levels. A bank with 10 per cent common equity Tier 1 capital can, in theory, withstand a 10 per cent hit to its risk-weighted assets before wiping out shareholder funds. That sounds reassuring. Yet "risk-weighted" is doing heavy work. Government bonds may carry a weight of zero, prime mortgages less than corporate loans. The numbers in the denominator reflect a model of the world.

Before the financial crisis, large European banks such as Deutsche Bank and BNP Paribas reported robust capital ratios based on internal models that treated certain assets as low risk. At the same time, their tangible leverage—the ratio of total assets to equity—was far higher. In good years, this produced impressive returns on equity. When markets reversed, thin capital was exposed. Losses ran through the balance sheet faster than models had anticipated. The implication is uncomfortable but important: capital ratios are part measurement, part performance. They signal safety but also invite optimisation. Banks restructure portfolios to minimise risk weights while maximising income. Regulators respond by adjusting definitions. It is a game played in spreadsheets, but its stakes are highways, hospitals, and jobs.

Contrast that with banks in jurisdictions that entered 2008 with more conservative leverage, such as Canada and Australia. Their capital cushions were thicker, their reliance on short-term wholesale funding lower. When global markets froze, they suffered but did not collapse. Depositors kept their faith; governments did not need to nationalise major institutions. The counter-example demonstrates that confidence can be earned, not just assumed. Yet it does not prove that high capital ratios alone are sufficient. They must be paired with credible asset valuations, transparent disclosures, and strong supervision. Numbers without trust are not enough.

Repo and capital operate together as a choreography. Haircuts on collateral define how much funding banks can obtain against their assets. Capital ratios define how much of that asset book is funded by loss-absorbing equity rather than flighty debt. Between the two, regulators and markets attempt to keep credit flowing. Raise haircuts too quickly, and funding vanishes. Demand too much capital too soon, and lending contracts. Move too slowly on either, and risk accumulates unseen. The ledger becomes a stage where confidence is continuously rehearsed and occasionally rewritten.

The most revealing episodes occur when accounting treatment collides with market judgement. Consider the

European banking system's handling of "held-to-maturity" bond portfolios during the sovereign crisis. By design, these securities were valued at cost rather than market price, on the assumption they would be held until repayment. On the balance sheet, losses were muted. In markets, yields on the same bonds spiked, implying sharp falls in value. Banks faced a dilemma. If they sold to raise liquidity, they would crystallise losses and reveal thinner capital. If they did not, markets would treat their published ratios with scepticism. The behaviour of bank share prices during this period—a steady drift down—showed how investors answered the question. They did not trust the book values. The implication is harsh: accounting can delay recognition of reality, but it cannot permanently suspend it.

Risk models add another layer. Value-at-Risk frameworks, widely adopted in the 1990s and 2000s, purported to estimate the maximum expected loss on a portfolio over a given period with a certain confidence level. A one-day 99 per cent VaR of £10 million suggests that, statistically, you should not lose more than that amount on more than one day in a hundred. Institutions such as J.P. Morgan codified these techniques. They became embedded in trading limits and capital allocation. Yet the models assumed that future price movements would resemble recent history. When the distribution of outcomes shifted, the models failed gracefully only on paper. In practice, they failed catastrophically. Losses far exceeded VaR estimates. The ledger lines that once signalled control suddenly signalled naivety.

Banking, then, sits on a knife-edge between measurement and myth. Haircuts, capital ratios, and risk models are indispensable. Without them, credit would be chaotic, and regulators blind. But they are not scientific constants. They are negotiated parameters in a social system. The more participants believe in them, the more accurate they become—until they do not.

The motif of the stage is useful here. Accounting is the set, with its rules and props. Collateral schedules, regulatory filings, capital buffers all inhabit this scenery. Confidence is the audience's willingness to suspend disbelief. As long as the audience believes the performance, the bank can borrow, lend, and transform maturities. When the audience starts checking the wiring behind the lights, the illusion weakens. A single rumour about asset quality, a leaked report about capital shortfalls, a sudden change in haircuts—these are like a curtain snagging mid-scene.

Recent episodes of stress in mid-sized banks have highlighted another complication: the speed at which confidence can now vanish. Social media compresses rumour cycles from days to hours. Mobile banking allows depositors to move funds with a swipe. In March 2023, Silicon Valley Bank's deposit outflows accelerated faster than any historical run. Liquidity ratios that appeared adequate on regulatory filings proved optimistic in the face of a digital stampede. The assumptions baked into these ratios—about how much cash customers might demand in a given period—no longer matched behaviour. The implication is sobering. Our metrics for risk and liquidity are backward-looking in a world where information and co-ordination move forward at unprecedented speed.

Some argue that stronger capital and more conservative collateral treatment are the answer: higher buffers, harsher haircuts. There is merit in this view. Better-prepared banks weather storms. Yet there is a limitation. Safety is not free. Extra capital must be funded. Tighter collateral rules restrict credit. The trade-off is political: how much potential growth is society willing to sacrifice for resilience? A system with no failures may be over-insured, stifling productive risk-taking. A system with frequent crises clearly underprices danger.

Others suggest more radical simplification. Replace complex internal models with blunt leverage caps. Restrict eligible collateral to a narrow set of truly safe assets. Reduce opportunities for regulatory arbitrage. This, too, has merit. But it pushes risk elsewhere—to capital markets, to shadow banks, to jurisdictions with lighter rules. Confidence may migrate, but its fragility remains.

We return, finally, to the image of the whiteboards at the New York Fed in September 2008. Lines between names, arrows showing exposures, numbers circled in red. Officials were not merely totalling losses. They were trying to reconstruct a map of confidence: who still trusted whom, on what terms, and for how long. The tools they reached for—central bank facilities, collateral guarantees, capital injections—were attempts to restage the performance, to persuade markets that the show could go on.

The question left hanging over every subsequent regulatory reform is simple but unresolved. Have we turned accounting into a more honest mirror of risk, or merely written a more elaborate script for the same, fragile play?

Payments, Fees, and Data

At 08:47 on 12 January 2018, the Australian Competition and Consumer Commission released a decision that sent quiet ripples through the global payments industry. The regulator fined Visa AU$18 million for practices that discouraged merchants from steering customers towards lower-cost debit networks. The case turned on a seemingly mundane detail: interchange fees of a few dozen basis points. Yet those slivers of revenue—collected on every tap, swipe, and online checkout—were substantial enough to provoke strategic behaviour by one of the world's largest payment networks. A microscopic friction, multiplied billions of times, had become a lucrative tide. The story revealed what insiders already knew. Payments are not free. Friction is gold dust.

Move from Sydney to London and the same pattern is visible. In June 2015, the European Commission capped interchange fees at 0.3 per cent for credit cards and 0.2 per cent for debit. The intention was clear: reduce the invisible tax on every transaction. Yet even after the cap, British merchants found that scheme fees—the charges networks levy on acquirers—began creeping upward. The friction migrated. Revenues hid in the shadows of complexity.

Payments sit at the junction of money and movement. Every time value is transferred, someone bears a cost. The question is who pays and who captures. Velocity is taxed not through explicit legislation but through the mechanics of networks. Card schemes, clearinghouses, correspondent banks, and digital wallets all extract slices, usually small enough to seem tolerable but large enough to matter in aggregate. The motif running through this terrain is the toll gate: always small, always inescapable.

Begin with interchange, the fee paid by the acquiring bank (the merchant's bank) to the issuing bank (the customer's bank). Visa and Mastercard set interchange schedules based on card type, merchant category, and transaction channel. A premium rewards card may attract 1.5 per cent; a basic debit card, far less. The justification is risk. Issuers argue that fraud exposure and credit provisioning require compensation. Yet risk is only part of the story. Interchange also funds cardholder perks, marketing campaigns, and network expansion. It is a pricing architecture designed to pull consumers into the system with rewards while passing most costs to merchants.

The implication is behavioural. When high-interchange cards offer generous points, consumers favour them. Merchants shoulder the bill but cannot easily steer shoppers to cheaper payment methods. In the United States, where interchange remains uncapped as of 2024, the average merchant discount rate often exceeds 2 per cent. Large retailers such as Walmart have pushed back for years, negotiating bespoke rates or litigating. Smaller businesses lack that leverage. The toll gate stands, and they walk through it daily.

Now consider float—the short period during which a bank or payment provider holds funds before releasing them to the recipient. In the 1970s, float generated material interest income for US banks as cheques took days to clear. Delays were technological and procedural. But even as clearing accelerated, the incentive to hold funds lingered. Until the Faster Payments Service became widely adopted in the UK after 2008, interbank transfers could still take hours or days. Banks earned interest on the float. The behaviour was subtle: structuring batch processing at certain times of day, delaying settlement to the next business cycle. Each delay was minor. Multiplied across millions of transactions, it became meaningful.

Regulators eventually pushed for real-time systems. The UK's Faster Payments, followed by similar projects in Scandinavia and Singapore, eroded float rents. Yet even these systems have soft edges. Faster Payments transactions can be throttled for fraud checks. Some banks process high-value transfers more cautiously. The float persists in pockets. It is thinner, less visible, but not extinct.

Data, however, is where the modern toll gate moves fastest. Payment data shows what people buy, when they buy, where they buy, and with which device. It reveals patterns that are commercially potent: grocery baskets that signal household composition; travel bookings that signal income; subscription patterns that signal loyalty or churn. Networks such as Mastercard and Visa aggregate vast flows of anonymised transaction data and sell analytics to retailers, advertisers, and financial institutions. In 2019, Mastercard's "Data & Services" segment reported revenue growth of more than 20 per cent year-on-year. The behaviour behind that figure is telling: swipes turned into signals, signals into dashboards.

The justification is efficiency. Merchants claim they can target promotions better; banks can manage fraud more effectively. These benefits are real. Yet the implication is concentration.

The entities that see the most transactions have the richest datasets. Competitors must either partner or rely on smaller samples. The toll gate has become informational.

For a second named example, consider India's Unified Payments Interface (UPI). Launched in 2016 by the National Payments Corporation of India, UPI eliminated interchange fees on peer-to-merchant payments for most categories. The network exploded, processing more than 10 billion transactions in October 2023. The price of zero fees produced a different dynamic. Large platforms such as PhonePe and Google Pay became dominant entry points. Their revenues depended less on fees and more on data, cross-selling, and favourable positioning. The friction shifted from money to attention. Instead of capturing a few basis points per transaction, platforms competed to capture the customer journey itself.

Some suggest this is progress. Zero-fee payments expand access. India's example demonstrates that ubiquity can be achieved when the toll gate is removed. But a credible counter-argument comes from Brazil's Pix. Launched by the Banco Central do Brasil in 2020, Pix also offers near-instant low-cost transfers. Yet Brazilian regulators imposed strict data governance rules and visibility limits on private platforms. Competition is more balanced. The limitation is clear: low cost does not guarantee low concentration. Payment networks thrive on network effects. Even free systems produce giants.

Reconciling these cases requires looking closely at incentives. When fees are high, banks and networks optimise for revenue capture. When fees approach zero, platforms optimise for engagement and data capture. In both scenarios, velocity is taxed. The currency of the tax changes; the logic does not.

The motif of the toll gate surfaces again in the architecture of clearinghouses. Automated Clearing House (ACH) networks in the United States, run by Nacha and the Federal Reserve, bundle payments into batches. Merchants pay fees to acquirers, who pay fees to processors, who pay fees to the network. Each step involves small charges. The system is reliable but not swift. Same-day ACH, introduced in 2016, sped up settlement, yet the underlying structure remains layered. The implication is inertia. Legacy systems accrete fees the way old roads accrete toll booths: added for specific purposes, rarely removed.

The UK's Bacs system exhibits similar traits. It processes more than six billion transactions annually. Fees are modest, but the system's three-day cycle introduces friction. Although Faster Payments covers many urgent transfers, Bacs remains essential for payroll and direct debits. Its rhythm structures behaviour. Companies schedule salaries around it. Households arrange bills. A three-day settlement window becomes a social habit. Remove it and decision-making changes. The toll gate shapes timing.

Digital wallets complicate the picture. When a consumer pays with Apple Pay or Google Pay, the transaction still runs over card rails. The wallet provider inserts itself as a new layer, gaining visibility into device and behaviour. Apple charges banks a small fee for each transaction. The friction is technical rather than monetary—control over the "secure element", integration with merchant apps, the ability to nudge consumer payment preferences. This is the toll gate as design. Banks cannot access NFC on iPhones without Apple's blessing. The implication is leverage. Control over hardware becomes control over payment choice.

A quieter yet potent friction sits in cross-border transfers. Correspondent banking networks connect more than 200 jurisdictions. Each link in the chain—from originating bank to correspondent to beneficiary bank—charges a fee. Foreign exchange spreads add another toll. The World Bank reported in 2022 that average remittance fees remained above 6 per cent. The behaviour behind that number is structural:

compliance checks, liquidity buffers in multiple currencies, legacy infrastructure, and market power in corridors with little competition. Migrant workers sending money from London to Lagos or Dubai to Dhaka pay not only for geography but for institutional distance. The toll gate spans continents.

A credible limitation in this discussion comes from instant cross-border pilot schemes such as those linking Singapore's PayNow and Thailand's PromptPay from 2021 onwards. Fees are low and transfers near-instant. Yet these are bilateral, not global. Scalability remains uncertain. They show what is possible but not what is yet typical.

Throughout all these examples, what unites them is that frictions shape behaviour long before they provoke complaint. A merchant deciding whether to accept premium credit cards. A small business delaying payroll by a day to avoid overdraft fees. A commuter choosing contactless over cash because tapping is faster, even if it costs more to the merchant. A migrant worker sending £400 instead of £500 because fees erode the total. These decisions are incremental but cumulative. Payments infrastructure shapes economic choreography.

The toll gate motif is also psychological. Fees that appear small numerically can loom large cognitively. A 1.5 per cent card fee feels negligible on a £10 purchase but punitive on a £10,000 invoice. As a result, some businesses add surcharges or offer discounts for bank transfers. Behaviour adjusts. Consumers faced with extra charges often switch methods. Regulation intervenes. Between 2018 and 2020, the UK banned most card surcharges. The intention was consumer protection; the implication was that merchants had to internalise card costs. Again, the friction did not vanish. It moved.

Data raises the most difficult questions. Who owns the exhaust of payment activity? When a bank observes that a customer spends £200 monthly at a particular supermarket, is that insight proprietary? When a payment network aggregates millions of such observations, does it hold a public good or a private asset? The European Union's GDPR offers one framework, emphasising consent and purpose limitation. But payments generate metadata that is difficult to disentangle. Device identifiers, location stamps, merchant category codes: all are technical necessities. They also form behavioural fingerprints.

Suppose regulators tighten rules on data monetisation. Networks may respond by adjusting interchange or scheme fees to compensate. Suppose regulators cap fees further. Networks may restrict access or reduce investment in fraud prevention. The tension is structural. Payments must be cheap, fast, secure, and inclusive. Achieving all four simultaneously requires trade-offs. Lower friction in one dimension often creates friction in another.

This leaves a final question, unresolved yet central. If the toll gates of payments cannot be removed, only redesigned, who should decide their placement?

Too Big to Fail, or Too Central to Replace

At 7:45 p.m. on 16 March 2008, inside the glass headquarters of the Federal Reserve Bank of New York, Timothy Geithner delivered a blunt message to JPMorgan Chase executives: they would take over Bear Stearns that night, and the Federal Reserve would provide a US$29 billion guarantee to make the deal possible. The alternative, he warned, was a collapse that could rupture global funding markets before Asian trading opened. Bear Stearns, a firm headquartered on Madison Avenue, had traded for US$172 a share in January 2007. Now it would be sold for US$2. **Two dollars.** A bank that had survived the Panic of 1907 was being dismantled over a weekend because the cost of letting it fail exceeded the cost of rescuing it. The message was unmistakable. Some institutions were not merely large. They were load-bearing.

That evening exposed an uncomfortable truth. When financial networks centralise risk and liquidity in a handful of nodes, those nodes gain a special kind of power. It is not formal power: Bear Stearns certainly did not ask to be rescued at humiliating terms. It is structural power: the ability, through one's position in the system, to dictate the menu of possible policy responses. In 2008, the choice presented to governments and central banks was not save or do nothing. It was save, or watch the system fail.

Years later, in March 2023, a different scene played out. Credit Suisse, a 167-year-old Swiss bank headquartered in Zurich, announced its liquidity position had deteriorated. Within days, its share price collapsed by more than 30 per cent. The Swiss National Bank extended a CHF 50 billion liquidity line. It was not enough. On 19 March 2023, UBS agreed to acquire Credit Suisse for CHF 3 billion, aided by a government guarantee of CHF 9 billion. Again, the calculus was structural. Policymakers feared that allowing Credit Suisse to collapse would destabilise European funding markets at a moment when global interest rates were rising. Size alone did not save the bank. But size ensured that its fate was a matter of national strategy, not corporate governance.

These events illustrate the motif that threads through this subchapter: the hinge. At certain scales, a bank becomes a hinge in the financial system. If the hinge breaks, the door falls. Public authorities must decide whether they can tolerate that outcome. Often they cannot. The hinge gains bargaining power.

Moral hazard is the conventional explanation. But the conventional explanation is too narrow. The deeper dynamic is connectivity: how many counterparties rely on an institution for settlement, collateral transformation, market-making, or liquidity provision. Bear Stearns mattered in 2008 because it held a vast portfolio of repurchase agreements and credit derivatives. Credit Suisse mattered in 2023 because it anchored Swiss payments, custody, and wealth management. Their balance sheets were dangerous. Their embeddedness was decisive.

The phrase "too big to fail" entered public discourse after 1984, when the US government facilitated a rescue of Continental Illinois, then the seventh-largest bank in the country. But the phenomenon predates the phrase. In 1866, the failure of Overend, Gurney & Company in London triggered panicked withdrawals across the banking system. The Bank of England, though reluctant, provided emergency liquidity to prevent wider collapse. Its reasoning was pragmatic: the City of London depended on Overend for discounting bills of exchange. Its failure compromised the machinery of Victorian commerce. Again, the hinge.

To understand the mechanics of this power, follow the behaviour of policymakers under stress. When an institution becomes systemically important, regulators treat it differently. They require thicker capital buffers, more stringent stress tests, and stricter reporting. Yet paradoxically, these measures also signal to markets that the institution is a pillar. Credit default swap spreads narrow. Funding costs fall. The institution acquires a subsidy embedded in expectations. That subsidy is invisible to the public but valuable to shareholders. The hinge becomes a magnet.

Consider JPMorgan Chase in the years following 2008. By 2014, the Financial Stability Board had designated it a Global Systemically Important Bank (G-SIB) with the highest "bucket" surcharge. This status required JPMorgan to hold additional capital. At the same time, the designation reinforced its reputation as the safest counterparty in global finance. Corporates placed deposits with it at low yields. Pension funds queued to transact with its prime brokerage. Its scale attracted more scale. Risk and advantage intertwined.

A credible counter-example emerges in the form of Lehman Brothers. It collapsed in September 2008 despite deep interconnectedness. Why was Lehman allowed to fail when Bear Stearns was not? The answer lies partly in politics and partly in architecture. Lehman's collateral was perceived as too weak to support a government guarantee; its balance sheet was opaque; its management had exhausted goodwill. The Federal Reserve judged it insolvent. Yet the aftermath proved the limitation of the assumption that markets could absorb the blow. Repo markets froze. Money market funds broke the buck. The hinge snapped. The door fell. Lehman's failure did not disprove systemic importance. It demonstrated the cost of ignoring it.

Reconcile the cases and the pattern resurfaces: policymakers misjudge which hinges cannot break, then adjust doctrine retroactively. In 2008, the US and UK governments extended deposit guarantees and launched emergency lending facilities. After 2023, Swiss regulators rewrote resolution frameworks within months. Systemic importance becomes visible only when it fails.

The bargaining power of the systemically important bank arises before any crisis. It manifests in the ordinary rhythms of policy dialogue. Large banks influence how payment regulations are drafted, how capital requirements are calibrated, how liquidity standards evolve. Not through open threats, but through knowledgeable persuasion. Regulators rely on these banks to understand market plumbing. When policymakers consider altering settlement times, collateral eligibility, or margining rules, they consult the institutions that dominate those markets. Expertise becomes leverage. The hinge speaks, and the door listens.

Behavioural evidence confirms this influence. In December 2011, during the eurozone sovereign debt crisis, the European Central Bank launched its first three-year Long-Term Refinancing Operation (LTRO). The programme aimed to stabilise banks by providing cheap funding. Large banks, including BNP Paribas and Banco Santander, borrowed heavily. Their decisions shaped the programme's effectiveness. Policymakers had designed a facility; systemically important banks decided its real-world usage. The hinge determined the rhythm.

Yet systemic importance is not only a matter of balance sheet size. It is a matter of functional centrality. In the UK, even mid-sized banks rely on a handful of clearing banks—such as Barclays, Lloyds, HSBC, and NatWest—for access to CHAPS, Faster Payments, and Bacs. These clearing banks process the lion's share of domestic payments. They hold settlement accounts at the Bank of England. They shape the pulse of national commerce. A failure among them would freeze wage payments, utility bills, tax receipts. Their centrality outstrips their size.

A limitation in the narrative arises from smaller jurisdictions. Iceland in 2008 let its entire banking system collapse. The government refused blanket guarantees. Yet even here, centrality dictated outcomes. Iceland could act radically because its banks' liabilities were largely offshore. The domestic payments system—while stressed—was small enough for the state to stabilise. The hinge held not because it was strong but because it was narrow. The lesson is not that systemic importance disappears. Rather, it varies by the reach of obligations.

This, then, guides the quiet motif of this subchapter: the hinge that strengthens as more weight rests on it. The hinge is invisible in normal times, felt keenly in stress, and debated fiercely afterward. Its strength is not chosen. It accrues.

When a bank becomes too central to replace, it acquires a subtle form of veto power. It can push back on regulatory proposals by warning—politely or implicitly—that certain rules may impair market functioning. Policymakers listen because the warning may be right. Market plumbing is intricate. A change in one valve can create pressure in another. Institutions positioned at the confluence of liquidity flows see these pressures early. That insight becomes soft influence.

The 2023 rescue of First Republic Bank in the United States, orchestrated by a coalition of larger banks that deposited US$30 billion to stabilise it, illustrates this dynamic. The coordination was remarkable. So was its signalling power. The large banks acted partly out of self-preservation; a destabilising run would have ricocheted through wholesale funding markets. Their intervention blurred the boundary between private initiative and public priority. The hinge flexed.

The forward question is stark and unresolved. If financial systems must occasionally rely on a few institutions to stabilise the many, how should that reliance be governed?

Chapter 4
Sovereignty and the Ledger

Shortly after 8 p.m. on a humid October evening in 2019, a thousand people gathered in a Hong Kong underpass illuminated only by phone screens. They held no banners, chanted no slogans. Instead, they passed money—small sums, whispered from one device to another—using prepaid cards and decentralised apps that left no personal trail. It was a fleeting gesture of solidarity, a way to support those who had lost their jobs after joining pro-democracy marches. But it was also something else: a quiet contest over who gets to see, permit, or prohibit the movement of value. As police scanners tracked bank transfers and retail surveillance tightened its net, the simple act of sending fifty dollars became a political choice. Standing beneath the concrete pillars, people realised that the line between a payment and a statement had collapsed.

This chapter begins in that half-lit tunnel because it captures the tension now running through every monetary system, from the world's richest democracies to its most brittle regimes. For centuries, states defined money by decree: a sovereign's promise stamped onto metal, later onto paper, eventually onto credit entries housed in regulated banks. Yet today, money increasingly moves through digital systems where enforcement is automatic, distributed, and sometimes beyond the reach of courts. What counts as money—and who decides—has become an open question. The machinery that settles our daily transactions is also the machinery that shapes our freedoms.

The contradiction is striking. In most countries, banknotes still bear the language of authority: the monarch's face, the central bank's signature, the assured phrase that this note is legal tender. But the money we use most often—the instant transfer between friends, the card tap at the supermarket, the cross-border remittance sent from an app—circulates not because it is legally mandated, but because networks agree to honour it. Visa's rules can, in practice, matter more than a government statute. Bitcoin's consensus algorithm can declare finality even when courts would disagree. The centre of gravity has shifted from decree to coordination. Sovereignty now shares the stage.

The stakes are obvious when friction enters the system. A donation blocked. A salary frozen. A transaction flagged because an algorithm misread context. These frictions rarely appear on a balance sheet, yet they shape the experience of money more powerfully than interest rates or inflation metrics. They remind us that every financial system carries an implicit social contract: the promise that value will flow unless there is a legitimate and proportionate reason to stop it. Break that promise and legitimacy erodes. Honour it and trust compounds.

But what constitutes a "legitimate reason" is increasingly contested. States frame digital monitoring as a defence against crime and terrorism. Citizens worry about mission creep and misuse. Payment networks insist on neutrality while exercising the discretion of private governors. Meanwhile, decentralised protocols resist censorship by design, embedding freedoms that are absolute when the world often requires nuance. The systems we build reflect the societies we want—or the societies we fear.

As we widen the lens, the chapter moves from domestic tension to global fault lines. Money does not cross borders freely; it moves through correspondent banks, each with its own risk calculus. A transfer from Beirut to Berlin can be delayed days because an intermediary in New York fears regulatory penalties. Sanctions policies, crafted to pressure states, now cascade to ordinary citizens who find their remittances blocked or their accounts de-risked out of existence. And yet, peer-to-peer networks increasingly route around these chokepoints, introducing new challenges: less visibility for regulators, more autonomy for users, greater uncertainty over jurisdiction. The old geography of money—defined by central banks, clearinghouses, and diplomatic alignments—is being overlaid by a decentralised geography shaped by code.

These tensions sharpen when money becomes programmable. A digital pound, a CBDC, a stablecoin—each offers efficiency and control. But they also usher in a world where policy can be applied at the individual level, not the institutional one. Instead of changing interest rates and hoping households respond, governments could, in principle, change the rules inside the money itself: restricting where it can be spent, setting expiry dates, automating tax collection. The design decisions are technical. Their effects are political. A future where every citizen becomes a policy endpoint is no longer theoretical; it is a design meeting waiting to happen.

Yet there is an alternative scenario unfolding at the edges. As self-custody tools become easier to use, individuals begin reclaiming a competence once reserved for institutions: the ability to hold value directly. A father in Buenos Aires saving in multisignature Bitcoin wallets to hedge against inflation. A student in Lagos storing stablecoins offline to avoid arbitrary bank freezes. A Syrian refugee crossing a border with her savings encoded in a seed phrase. These stories complicate the simplistic debate between state control and crypto freedom. They reveal the human stakes: the right to hold and move value without permission, weighed against the need to maintain a functioning public order.

Threaded through all of this is a subtle motif: the ledger as a mirror. Whether maintained by a central bank or a decentralised network, a ledger reflects choices about power, visibility, and consequence. A system that records everything extends safety to some and vulnerability to others. A system that records nothing protects dissidents and criminals alike.

The balance is delicate. Every society must decide where to place its mirror—and how much of itself it is willing to see.

This chapter explores that balance with care and candour. It examines the boundary between legal tender and social tender: the difference between what the law says we must accept and what people actually trust. It investigates the shifting terrain of privacy, where anonymity can be a democratic safeguard or a tool for evasion. It charts the geopolitical use of payment networks as instruments of influence. And it confronts the uncomfortable possibility that, as money becomes programmable, citizens may find themselves not only protected by the state but increasingly governed through their transactions.

The questions that follow are not abstractions. They shape everyday life. Who decides when a payment is "allowed"? Who audits the auditors? What happens when two forms of authority—state law and network consensus—collide? And what rights does a citizen have when the ledger becomes the battlefield?

The path through these questions is neither simple nor predictable. But it matters deeply. For in the end, sovereignty is not a slogan or a flag. It is the power to define finality: to decide what counts, who counts, and whose rules prevail when systems disagree.

The pages ahead pull this tension into focus. They reveal the contest over the ledger—not as a technical debate, but as the story of modern citizenship itself.

What Counts as Money

On 7 September 2021, in San Salvador's Plaza Gerardo Barrios, President Nayib Bukele stood before a crowd and declared Bitcoin legal tender in El Salvador. The *Ley Bitcoin*, passed three months earlier, required merchants to accept bitcoin alongside the US dollar. ATMs branded "Chivo" flickered to life across the capital. International headlines spoke of a brave experiment, a sovereign pivot towards stateless money. But a few blocks away, outside a small bakery, the scene was more prosaic. A customer held out his phone to pay in bitcoin. The owner shook her head and pointed to a cardboard sign: "No crypto. Cash only." On paper, Bitcoin was money. At the counter, it was not. The law said *you must accept this.* The baker replied, quietly but firmly, *I will not.*

That dissonance captures the puzzle at the heart of this subchapter. States declare certain tokens "legal tender", fit and final for the discharge of debts. Yet the money that actually changes hands—the "social tender" people trust and use—often obeys a different authority. Argentines quote rents in US dollars despite peso legal tender laws. Zimbabweans hoard South African rand and dollars even when their government insists on local notes. Salvadoran bakers refuse the currency their president champions. The core question is disarmingly simple: when law and practice diverge, what *really* counts as money?

A quiet motif runs through these examples: the question at the till. *Will you take this?* The answer decides more than any statute.

Legal tender, in its narrow sense, is a courtroom concept. It determines what a creditor must accept if a debtor offers payment under the law. If you owe sterling in the United Kingdom and offer Bank of England notes, a court will treat the debt as satisfied. But legal tender status does not guarantee everyday use. Scottish banknotes are not technically legal tender anywhere in the UK, yet few shopkeepers in Glasgow hesitate to accept them. No Act of Parliament forced that outcome. Shared practice did.

This distinction becomes sharper as money detaches from physical tokens. Most of what we call money now is a ledger entry at a bank or payment provider. Its acceptability depends less on the statute book and more on the perceived reliability of the institution and the network. When you send a Faster Payment from Manchester to Bristol, neither party checks the Coinage Act. They trust that the system will credit one account and debit another. The *social tender* here is not the pound as defined in law, but the bank balance as implemented in code and contracts.

Bitcoin and other cryptocurrencies enter this landscape as a third category. They are rarely legal tender; El Salvador and the Central African Republic are exceptions, not rules. Yet they may function as social tender in niche communities: online marketplaces, remittance corridors, informal savings clubs. Their "legal" status oscillates between asset, commodity, and property depending on jurisdiction. Courts in England and Wales, for instance, recognised cryptoassets as property in the 2019 case *AA v Persons Unknown*, allowing them to be subject to injunctions and trusts. The ledger does not care. It records only keys and signatures.

The friction arises when these layers collide. Imagine a British court ordering the reversal of a fraudulent bank transfer. In the conventional system, enforcement is straightforward: judges can compel banks to debit and credit ledgers under threat of sanction. Finality is legal, not technical. Now imagine the same court ordering the reversal of a bitcoin transaction. The Bitcoin network will not oblige. No judge can force nodes to rewrite history. The most a court can do is compel identified parties to send compensating transactions. Finality remains with the chain. Legal authority can reallocate loss, but it cannot flip the bits.

That asymmetry becomes philosophical when communities decide to override code collectively. The 2016 "DAO hack" on Ethereum is the canonical case. A smart contract—the DAO—misdirected around 3.6 million ether due to a vulnerability. The contract behaved "as coded"; funds moved in accordance with its logic. Yet many in the Ethereum community judged the outcome unacceptable. After debate, a majority agreed to implement a hard fork that returned the funds, effectively editing the ledger's history. A minority objected, arguing that "code is law", and continued the original chain as Ethereum Classic. Two ledgers emerged from one event, each claiming legitimacy. Courts were spectators. Finality was decided by network consensus and market preference.

Name what happened clearly. Social tender split. The community that valued corrective justice followed the forked chain. The community that valued strict immutability stayed with the original. Exchanges, developers, and users cast votes through code and price. The question at the till reappeared in a more abstract form: *Which chain will you take as payment?* The answer settled the matter.

Yet states have not ceded their role in defining money. They still legislate legal tender; they still control tax obligations. You may choose to denominate a contract in Bitcoin, but you cannot pay HMRC in it. If you sell an asset for ether, the taxman measures your gain in pounds. That power to choose the unit of account, and to demand settlement in specific forms, is a core component of monetary sovereignty. It binds the legal and fiscal system together. Network consensus can define what is technically valid. Only the state can decide what discharges your duty to it.

There are, however, moments when state power over money falters visibly. In November 2016, India's government announced the demonetisation of ₹500 and ₹1,000 rupee notes, rendering them invalid overnight as legal tender for most purposes. Citizens queued outside banks to exchange old notes for new ones. Officially, the rupee remained legal tender; practically, certain forms of it had been excommunicated. Yet within weeks, reports emerged of informal markets still accepting old notes at discounts, particularly in rural areas with limited access to banks. Social tender did not vanish on command. People accepted what they believed others would accept soon after, betting that someone further along the chain would manage the conversion. The law set the boundary; social necessity stretched it.

Contrast that with dollarisation episodes. In Ecuador, after the sucre collapsed, the US dollar became legal tender by decree in March 2000. Yet usage had already spread informally as citizens fled the national currency. Legal tender status ratified existing behaviour. Something similar can be seen in hyperinflationary periods across Latin America and Africa, where supermarkets quietly reprice goods in dollars even while tills nominally accept local notes. The law lags the till.

The motif that emerges is not "law versus markets", but an ongoing negotiation. Legal tender laws express the state's claim about what should count as money. Social tender practices express the population's verdict on what *does* count. Network consensus adds a third voice: what the machines will recognise as valid. When these voices harmonise, money feels uncontroversial. When they clash, monetary disputes become constitutional.

These disputes surface with particular force around the notion of finality. In the banking system, finality is layered. A card payment can be reversed through chargeback rules; a Faster Payment, once cleared, is practically irreversible but can still be unwound by coordinated action between banks under legal instruction. In high-value systems like CHAPS or Fedwire, settlement is defined as "final and irrevocable" by statute, often anchored in settlement finality directives. Yet even these systems sit under legal umbrellas. Bankruptcy courts can claw back certain transfers; fraud can void apparent consent.

Blockchains offer a different notion of finality: probabilistic and protocol-defined. A Bitcoin transaction is considered effectively final after, say, six blocks. An Ethereum transaction gains confidence after a few confirmations or after checkpointing under proof-of-stake. These definitions are emergent. They are based on economic assumptions about how costly it would be to rewrite history, not on any legal doctrine. If a theft occurs, the chain will confirm it; the protocol has no concept of "illegitimate intent". Law and code diverge on the meaning of a valid transfer.

Cases like Mt. Gox's bankruptcy in Tokyo in 2014 expose the gap. The exchange had lost hundreds of thousands of bitcoins. Japanese courts oversaw liquidation and distribution. But the network itself did nothing to mark or reverse stolen coins. Bitcoins once belonging to Mt. Gox customers continued to move through addresses neutral to their origin. Some coins seized by law enforcement were auctioned; others disappeared into mixers. For the court, claims were denominated and settled in yen. For the network, all that existed were UTXOs with changing keys. Two ledgers, two notions of restitution.

As central banks explore digital currencies, they confront this gap head-on. A retail central bank digital currency (CBDC) would encode legal tender directly into a programmable ledger. The same institution that defines legal tender would operate the core network. In principle, this collapses the distinction between decree and settlement: what the ledger records *is* what the law recognises. Yet design choices still matter. Will the CBDC support offline transfers? Will it allow anonymity up to certain thresholds, like cash? Will it permit unilateral reversal by administrators? Each choice answers the question of who enforces finality.

Private stablecoins offer a partial inversion. Their issuers promise 1:1 backing with sovereign currency, but the ledger that tracks claims is proprietary. When a regulator orders a freeze on an address—as has happened with Tether and USD Coin—the smart contract can blacklist it. Network consensus accepts the transaction as valid; the contract layer imposes a veto. Here, finality becomes conditional. The question at the till shifts again: *Will the contract honour this receipt?*

A credible counter-example lies in systems that try to maximise independence from both state and issuer. Privacy-focused cryptocurrencies such as Monero or Zcash aim to obscure transaction details while preserving decentralised verification. They eschew central blacklists; they resist retroactive censorship. Yet their social tender remains limited. Major exchanges delist them under regulatory pressure. Merchants fear regulatory scrutiny. Users, weighing anonymity against conversion friction, often choose more visible assets. Sovereignty in code collides with sovereignty in law.

Reconciliation does not come from choosing a camp. It comes from recognising that money is a layered institution. At one layer, code enforces who can spend which units and how often. At another, law defines which of those units discharge obligations to the state and to one another. At a third, social norms decide what people will accept in the absence of compulsion. Any proposed reform—whether a CBDC design, a new stablecoin, or a protocol upgrade—must navigate all three.

We return, finally, to the baker in San Salvador, standing beneath a poster that proclaims Bitcoin "el dinero del futuro". For her, the decision at the till is pragmatic. Dollars pay suppliers. Dollars pay rent. Bitcoin is volatile, technically intimidating, and costly to convert. Her answer to the silent question—*Will you take this?*—remains no. But the story does not end at the bakery door. Around her, software continues to evolve, laws continue to experiment, crises continue to unsettle assumptions about what money should be.

The unresolved tension sits where it began: between the statute, the ledger, and the hand that must choose what to accept. When courts and code disagree about finality, whose judgement should prevail—and how do we ensure that the people using money, rather than merely administering it, have a say in the answer?

Privacy, Surveillance, and Rights

On 14 February 2022, the Royal Canadian Mounted Police issued an order naming 34 cryptocurrency addresses linked to donations supporting the "Freedom Convoy" protests in Ottawa. The instruction, grounded in emergency powers invoked that week by Prime Minister Justin Trudeau, obliged payment processors and financial institutions to freeze funds associated with the movement. Within hours, banks limited access to several accounts; some donors said they could not pay rent. Yet a handful of bitcoin transfers still reached organisers through peer-to-peer exchanges, bypassing intermediaries but not escaping scrutiny. Blockchain analytics firms traced flows; journalists published wallet histories; police obtained warrants. A tool designed to offer autonomy became a public ledger of political allegiance. Privacy served as shield for donors seeking to bypass banks. Auditability served as sword in the state's hand.

The friction felt uncanny because it compressed two worlds that rarely collide so starkly. Cash, for most of its history, has offered anonymity by default. A £20 note carries no memory of its previous holders. A bitcoin UTXO, by contrast, remembers every hop since genesis. Both can fund dissent, yet only one exposes each prior step to forensic inspection. The protest-donation episode revealed what many technologists understand abstractly but few citizens feel viscerally: the transition from physical money to digital ledgers is not merely a shift in format. It is a reconfiguration of rights. It changes who can see, who can block, and who can judge.

A quiet motif threads through this subchapter: the record that cannot forget. Every payment system decides how much to remember. That design choice shapes civic space.

Cash anonymity emerged not from a philosophy but from material constraints. A banknote printed by the Bank of England circulates without a central log of holders. When one person hands another a note in Birmingham, no registry measures the transfer. That absence of memory allows private acts: tipping, donating, settling small debts, supporting causes. It also allows illicit trade. Legislators know this, yet they hesitate to abolish cash entirely because it occupies a symbolic and practical place in democratic societies. It allows participation without identification.

Digital payments invert that logic. A debit card purchase at a shop in Leeds generates a timestamp, merchant code, amount, card identifier, and bank metadata. The merchant gains insight into purchasing patterns. The bank sees account behaviour. The card network aggregates flows across regions. Regulators may request data. Each transfer leaves a trail. This is not inherently malign. Fraud detection depends on it. Chargebacks rely on it. Anti-money-laundering frameworks, built since the 1980s, assume it. But the visibility comes with consequences: financial identity becomes a proxy for civic identity, and power accrues to those who can read or restrict the ledger.

Cryptocurrencies attempt to blend the qualities of cash and digital payments, and in doing so create a hybrid: pseudonymity. Bitcoin addresses do not carry names, but they broadcast transactions publicly. Chainalysis, CipherTrace, and other firms (reports from Chainalysis, 2022) have shown that clustering heuristics, IP data, and exchange compliance routines can link addresses to individuals with striking accuracy. Pseudonymity is brittle. A single transaction to a regulated exchange can reveal the owner's cluster. The protest donors learned this when police orders reached exchanges, compelling them to freeze funds associated with flagged addresses.

Yet privacy-focused cryptocurrencies present a counter-example. Monero, launched in 2014, obscures senders, receivers, and amounts through ring signatures and stealth addresses. Zcash, introduced in 2016, uses zk-SNARKs to allow shielded transactions that hide counterparties entirely while preserving verifiability. These systems seek to preserve cash-like anonymity in digital form. But they face regulatory and practical hurdles. Major exchanges delisted some of these assets in 2020–2021 due to compliance risks. Their liquidity is lower; their merchant acceptance is limited. The desire for privacy meets the architecture of oversight.

The tension crystallises in state-backed digital currency projects. China's e-CNY pilots, reported by the People's Bank of China in 2021, integrate what officials call "controllable anonymity"—small transactions may remain pseudonymous, but authorities can inspect flows at will. The architecture embeds auditability as a feature, not a side effect. The European Central Bank's exploratory work on a digital euro, outlined in 2022, entertains tiered privacy: offline low-value payments might mimic cash anonymity, while online high-value transfers would be fully traceable. The design is political. It weighs civil liberties against enforcement imperatives.

Showing these dynamics requires naming specific behaviours. When Canadian banks froze donor accounts, customers changed withdrawal patterns, as documented in February 2022 parliamentary committee transcripts. Some withdrew savings pre-emptively, fearing additional freezes. Merchants in Ottawa reported lower card usage around protest zones, anticipating scrutiny. The data trail shaped conduct. By contrast, in Hong Kong's 2019 protests, citizens rushed to purchase single-use transport cards—the Octopus—using cash to avoid creating trip logs. Tens of thousands queued at MTR stations. The anonymity of cash offered tactical cover. People adapted to the memory of the ledger.

A limitation complicates any narrative of privacy as virtue and auditability as vice: opaque systems can shield corruption, tax evasion, and violent crime. Transparency champions point to the Panama Papers (ICIJ, 2016) and the 1MDB scandal to argue that secrecy enables state-level theft. They see chain auditability as a democratic tool. They note that Russia's attempts to evade sanctions in 2022 faced constraints because blockchain flows were visible, and compliance teams at exchanges could freeze assets. Privacy, in their telling, is a sword in the hands of kleptocrats. They are not entirely wrong.

Reconciliation lies in proportionality. Privacy should not default to opacity; auditability should not default to dragnets. The point is not to sanctify one or demonise the other but to measure what they permit and prohibit. A system that records every transaction in perpetuity, tied to real identities, risks chilling dissent. A system that erases all traces risks enabling coercion by those operating outside the rule of law. The question is not "Should we have privacy?" but "Who controls it, and under what rules?"

Consider the European Union's General Data Protection Regulation (GDPR), implemented in 2018. It enshrines data minimisation and purpose limitation. Payment providers must document why they store data and how long they retain it. But GDPR collides with blockchain design. Data recorded on-chain is, by definition, hard to erase. The UK Information Commissioner's Office flagged this in 2019, noting the tension between immutability and the right to rectification. Law seeks forgetting. Code insists on memory.

The quiet motif returns—the record that cannot forget. When protesters in Canada used bitcoin, the blockchain logged their support. When authorities analysed flows, they could reconstruct events. In systems built for durability, memory becomes power. The question is who wields it.

Physical cash provides a foil. In 2020, during Belarus's protests against Alexander Lukashenko, activists distributed funds in banknotes to support striking workers. The regime struggled to trace donors. Cash insulated networks of solidarity. But when activists abroad attempted to send crypto donations via Bitcoin and Ethereum, state-aligned hackers targeted local wallets. Transparency became attack surface. Organisers later turned to privacy protocols, but liquidity constraints and technical complexity limited reach. The means of transfer shaped the movement's resilience.

Even everyday settings reveal the stakes. When supermarkets in London roll out loyalty apps that track item-level purchases, they price targeted discounts based on personal profiles. That data profile informs credit decisions, insurance premiums, and risk scoring. A purchase becomes a datapoint. Behaviour adjusts. People choose cash to avoid leaving traces of certain buys—medication, reading material, gifts—precisely because privacy carries social meaning. Surveillance is not abstract; it is lived.

A second example comes from Kenya's M-Pesa system, launched by Safaricom in 2007. Its logs record transaction metadata across millions of users. Researchers analysing anonymised M-Pesa data in 2016 observed how users in Nairobi sent micro-transfers to friends as informal insurance. The system's memory enabled agents of the state or private firms to construct detailed social graphs. It also allowed humanitarian agencies to deliver cash assistance with low leakage. Memory helped and harmed. The balance shifted with governance.

A credible counterpoint must be acknowledged: many citizens welcome auditability when it detects fraud, corruption, or abuse. Estonia's e-government system, built since the early 2000s, logs access to personal records. Citizens can view who accessed their data. Transparency fosters trust because surveillance runs both ways. The system shows that auditability can serve rights as well as control. Yet Estonia's model relies on legal guardrails and civic consensus. It is a rare case, not a universal blueprint.

Where does this leave the design of monetary systems? The implication is stark. The spectrum from cash anonymity to complete auditability is not merely technical. It defines the boundaries of civic freedom. It determines whether dissenters can donate without fear, whether minorities can transact without scrutiny, whether states can monitor flows at scale. The design of a CBDC or the policy of a payments firm becomes a human rights question.

One must also ask who sets defaults. If privacy requires specialist knowledge—VPNs, mixers, shielded pools, hardware wallets—only the technically adept will benefit. If auditability is frictionless and pervasive, chilling effects spread. Defaults matter because they shape the ordinary, not the exceptional.

The unresolved tension hangs over the protest-donation example. If a state deems a movement illegitimate, how far should it reach into financial rails to suppress support? Should donors' identities be exposed? Should platforms be intermediaries of political enforcement? Alternatively, if privacy tools enable harmful actors to move funds invisibly, how should societies respond without dismantling legitimate protections for dissent?

The question returns to the motif: the record that cannot forget. Should money remember this much?

Sanctions and Borders

On 26 February 2022, two days after Russian troops crossed into Ukraine, the SWIFT cooperative in Brussels removed several Russian banks from its messaging network. The measure, announced jointly by the European Union, the United States, Canada, and the United Kingdom, did not fire a single weapon. Yet within hours Russian importers struggled to settle invoices; energy traders scrambled to reroute flows; families found remittances delayed or blocked. Banks in

Moscow could still hold dollars. They could still hold euros. What they could not do—without SWIFT—was *signal* reliably across borders. A payment rail had become a political instrument. The sanction did not freeze assets directly; it severed conversational lines between institutions. Cutting a line changed the battle.

This was not the first time geopolitics bent the rails. In 2012, when the United States Treasury pressed SWIFT to disconnect Iranian banks over the country's nuclear programme, Tehran experienced what local economists called an "import choke." Hospitals faced shortages of specialised drugs; shipping companies struggled to clear letters of credit; small firms resorted to cash couriers. A technical exclusion became a broad coercive tool. A system built to settle obligations had become a frontier of statecraft.

The motif that runs quietly through this subchapter—the chokepoint—appears early. Every payment system, from SWIFT to Visa to Bitcoin's mempool, contains points of concentrated control. Those points define who can be stopped, who can adapt, and who navigates around blockades.

Correspondent banking is the architecture that gives chokepoints their reach. When a bank in Lagos wants to send dollars to a supplier in Singapore, it typically uses a correspondent in New York. That correspondent sits under United States jurisdiction. It must respect the Office of Foreign Assets Control's sanctions list. If OFAC designates a Nigerian firm, the American correspondent may freeze flows or terminate relationships. The designation radiates outward, shaping decisions thousands of miles away. This is not abstract. In 2015, several Caribbean banks lost access to correspondent accounts when American peers stopped servicing them—so-called "de-risking." Remittance companies in Belize and Guyana saw long delays. The World Bank reported that transaction costs rose, and smaller money service businesses closed. A regulatory choice in one jurisdiction rippled through entire regions.

Yet correspondent networks are not omnipotent. Their limits were exposed in Venezuela. When the Maduro government faced financial restrictions from the United States in 2017, it resorted to gold shipments to Turkey as reported by Turkish and Venezuelan trade data. Bullion moved physically, bypassing dollar rails. This was cumbersome and expensive, but it shows that sanctions can be navigated when states are willing to bear cost and risk. The chokepoint bends, not breaks.

The emergence of cryptocurrencies added a new route. In 2021, the Iranian government acknowledged that bitcoin miners could export electricity indirectly by mining coins and selling them abroad. Hash rate became a geopolitical valve. Regulators in the United States worried that sanctioned entities might use crypto to soften the impact of embargoes. Yet blockchain's visibility introduced counterweights. When North Korean hackers stole $620 million in March 2022 from the Ronin network (according to the FBI), exchanges froze funds as they attempted to pass through mixers. The ledger remembered too much for the escape to be clean. The chokepoint shifted from correspondent banks to liquidity providers.

A second example illustrates the dynamic. After Russia's 2022 invasion, Ukrainian civil society organisations received millions of pounds' worth of crypto donations within weeks, routed through wallets not easily constrained by traditional sanctions filters. Humanitarian aid reached Kyiv even when card processors experienced outages. Peer-to-peer rails offered speed. But they did not fully escape geopolitics: regulators later pressured exchanges to block Russian users more broadly, prompting questions over jurisdiction and fairness. Sanctions seeped into the decentralised realm because liquidity funnels back into regulated off-ramps.

A credible counter-example tempers the narrative of bypass. In October 2021, the Financial Action Task Force reported that crypto's global share in sanctions evasion remained small relative to traditional methods like trade-based money laundering. Large-scale illicit flows still favour mispriced invoices, shell firms, and cooperative intermediaries. Digital currency, at scale, introduces traceability and volatility risks that deter sustained use. The limitation is material: crypto helps individuals cross barriers, but states facing full-spectrum sanctions still rely on trade allies, clandestine shipping, or natural resource swaps.

To reconcile this, we must measure behaviours, not myths. When Nigerian youths in Lagos used bitcoin during the 2020 EndSARS protests to circumvent frozen bank accounts, they moved small, frequent transfers using mobile apps. The visible behaviour was tactical: volunteers used QR codes to receive funds before converting them to naira through peer intermediaries. By contrast, when Russian entities sought to move billions after the 2022 sanctions, they confronted liquidity limits: major exchanges implemented geo-blocks; OTC desks required enhanced due diligence; stablecoin issuers froze flagged addresses. Scale meets scrutiny.

A motif returns: the chokepoint. What appears decentralised still funnels through narrow bridges—exchanges, stablecoin issuers, banking partners, or electricity grids. Control rarely disappears; it migrates.

Sanctions regimes thrive on predictability. OFAC lists published in Washington translate into automated filters at HSBC in London, DBS in Singapore, and Banco do Brasil in São Paulo. The SWIFT message format MT103 includes compliance codes that structure how banks flag suspicious transactions. When a payment halts, the behaviour is visible: traders renegotiate contracts; shippers demand upfront cash; insurers reassess routes. Sanctions change prices. They change routes. They change trust.

But peer-to-peer flows challenge predictability. In Afghanistan in late 2021, after the Taliban takeover triggered the freeze of central bank reserves and disruption of commercial banking, families turned to hawala networks and occasionally to stablecoins like USDT. Hawala agents in Dubai and Istanbul settled accounts using informal ledgers, phone calls, and remittances disguised as trade. These systems operate outside correspondent chains. Their resilience stems from social trust rather than legal frameworks. They can route around chokepoints, but at the cost of opacity and potential exploitation. The bypass helps those excluded by geopolitics but risks enabling networks with fewer safeguards.

A second thread appears: the substitution of rails. When formal routes choke, informal ones thicken. When sanctions target digital wallets, users shift to community trust. When correspondent banks withdraw from risk, fintechs and money transfer operators fill gaps. Payment systems adapt like rivers around rocks.

The counterpoint acknowledges danger. Informal rails can mask funding for violent groups. Governments fear that excessive decentralisation weakens legitimate enforcement. The challenge is proportionality. Excessive sanctions create humanitarian fallout. Insufficient oversight invites abuse.

The policy dilemma touches the structure of global finance. The dollar's dominance is tied to the depth of U.S. capital markets and the global reach of American correspondent banks. This gives Washington leverage. But it also encourages sanctioned states to seek alternatives: China's Cross-Border Interbank Payment System (CIPS), launched in 2015, offers yuan-based settlement. Usage remains modest, but growth during 2022–2023 signals geopolitical intent. Russia, cut off from many Western rails, deepened integration with CIPS and explored ruble-yuan settlement for energy. Here sanctions accelerate financial fragmentation.

Yet even alternative rails have chokepoints. CIPS still uses SWIFT for messaging in many transactions. It depends on Chinese regulatory oversight. Network power persists. The question becomes whose rules travel across borders, not whether rules travel.

Alongside state projects, decentralised finance proposes a different escape: replacing correspondent banks with smart contracts. But here too chokepoints appear. Stablecoins rely on issuers who can freeze assets. Decentralised exchanges rely on price oracles. Bridges rely on validators. Each point introduces jurisdiction, liability, or influence. Even Bitcoin, the archetype of neutrality, faces practical chokepoints when users convert to fiat, use centralised custodians, or rely on miners concentrated in specific regions.

The tension is structural. Payment rails are built to enforce constraints—credit limits, identity checks, settlement windows. Geopolitics repurposes those constraints for strategic ends. Peer-to-peer systems try to dissolve points of control but create new surfaces for pressure. The shape changes. The logic persists.

Behaviour reveals truth. Traders use workaround currencies. Migrant workers choose mobile money. Protesters adopt crypto. Governments block IP ranges. Exchanges freeze addresses. Each action draws a map of how rules travel and how people navigate them.

The chokepoint motif arrives once more. Borders exist not only on land but in ledgers. Every sanction seeks to redraw those borders. Every innovation seeks to redraw them again.

A final tension remains unresolved. If financial networks become more decentralised, do sanctions lose teeth, leaving states with fewer peaceful tools for coercion and more incentive for force? Or does radical transparency in digital systems create new enforcement models that pressure rogue actors while sparing civilians? The answer depends on choices yet to be made. The map of money is being redrawn. The chokepoints are shifting. Who controls the next one?

The Citizen as Counterparty

In October 2020, shoppers in Shenzhen queued outside brightly lit supermarkets clutching their phones, not their wallets. The People's Bank of China had distributed digital "red packets" of e-CNY to 50,000 residents in a public lottery. Each packet contained 200 yuan, preloaded into an official app. The terms were precise: spend within a fortnight, at designated merchants inside a specific district, or the funds would vanish. At the till, QR codes flashed and balances fell to zero exactly as the software decreed. A familiar festival ritual had been recast as a live pilot of programmable money. Policy did not stop at the central bank's balance sheet. It reached directly into a shopper's pocket. One line of code sufficed.

That experiment crystallised a shift. Historically, citizens encountered monetary policy indirectly. Central banks nudged interest rates; governments changed tax rules. The effects filtered through banks, employers, and prices. You were never the direct counterparty of the central bank. With programmable digital currencies—whether public like e-CNY or private like major stablecoins—the relationship changes. Code can attach conditions to money itself: where it can be spent, when it expires, which addresses it may touch. The citizen is no longer just a user of money. They become an endpoint in a networked policy system.

A quiet motif runs through this terrain: the switch. Who holds it, who can flip it, and how visible its wiring is. Every design choice in programmable money decides which switches exist and who controls them.

Programmability promises precision. Governments can target stimulus at sectors they deem vulnerable, as Chinese municipalities did in 2020–2021 by issuing expiring digital vouchers usable only for retail, not speculative investments. The behaviour was concrete: citizens rushed to book restaurants and buy consumer goods before the deadline. Local officials measured uptake rates and sales spikes. The implication is alluring for policymakers. Instead of hoping that a blanket rate cut will trickle into the "real economy", they can script money to nudge specific actions—spend here, not there; spend now, not later.

Yet the same mechanism can encode constraint. Imagine a fuel subsidy paid in a CBDC that cannot be used for air travel. Technically trivial. Or a pandemic support payment that cannot be spent on gambling apps. Already contemplated. Each rule may be defensible when considered alone. But taken together, they transform the character of money. It ceases to be a general-purpose claim on resources and becomes a menu of authorised behaviours. The citizen at the till, or at the online checkout, discovers that the switch is not in their hands.

Blacklists make the switch explicit. In February 2022, when the Canadian government invoked the Emergencies Act to respond to the Ottawa protests, banks received lists of names and were instructed to freeze accounts without a court order. Card transactions failed. Direct debits bounced. Individuals experienced policy not as a distant speech but as a silent refusal at point of use. At the same moment, cryptocurrency issuers and exchanges received orders naming specific addresses. The stablecoin issuer Tether has, since 2017, repeatedly blacklisted addresses associated with hacks or sanctions; Circle's USD Coin contract similarly supports freezing specific accounts. The behaviour is visible on-chain: balances that can no longer move, tokens trapped by a function call.

These are not theoretical capacities. They are operational tools. They show how design hard-wires power. A blacklist in a smart contract, or in a CBDC core system, is a standing instruction: *funds belonging to identities on this list do not behave like other funds.* Once this capability exists, the political question is no longer *can* we freeze X, but *when* and *for whom.*

Advocates of strong enforcement argue that such switches are necessary. They point to terrorist financing, child exploitation, large-scale fraud. Here, programmable blacklists and real-time controls can prevent harm before it occurs, rather than merely punishing it afterwards. An address linked to a ransomware gang can be blocked across compliant platforms. A stolen stablecoin haul can be frozen within minutes of a hack. The citizen as counterparty benefits as victim rather than suffers as suspect.

But the same architecture scales effortlessly to other priorities. A government facing protests can pressure payment providers to classify certain groups as high risk. A tax authority can require smart contracts to withhold VAT automatically at source, leaving entrepreneurs with no room to manage timing. A welfare agency can restrict benefits to specific merchant categories, effectively imposing a moral judgement on consumption. The switch moves closer to the individual, and the individual's margin of discretion narrows.

Here, self-custody appears as counterweight. When citizens hold private keys directly—whether for Bitcoin, ether, or self-hosted stablecoins—they reduce their exposure to institutional switches. A hardware wallet in a drawer in Buenos Aires, loaded with savings, cannot be frozen by a foreign regulator. A multisignature setup shared between family members in Lagos resists unilateral seizure. Small but growing communities teach one another how to back up seed phrases, verify addresses, and avoid phishing attacks. The behaviour is quietly radical. People learn to manage a role previously reserved for banks: custody.

Self-custody is not only a technical act. It is a form of civic competence. It demands understanding of risk, inheritance planning, operational security. It encourages questions once unasked: suppose my government imposes capital controls; suppose my bank fails; suppose my cause becomes unpopular—how do I keep value accessible? The citizen as counterparty uses tools to maintain agency rather than relying on institutional goodwill.

Yet self-custody has hard limits. Many people do not want or cannot safely bear the burden. Loss of keys means loss of funds. Social engineering attacks target individuals who lack professional defence teams. During Nigeria's 2021 crackdown on bank accounts linked to the EndSARS movement, activists turned to Bitcoin and stablecoins. Some managed peer-to-peer sales successfully. Others fell prey to fraudsters posing as legitimate counterparties. Technical power without social infrastructure can damage the very communities it intends to protect.

Reconciling these poles reveals a spectrum rather than a binary. At one end lie fully custodial systems: CBDC wallets, neobanks, super-apps where policy can reach individuals cheaply and instantly. At the other end lie self-custody tools: cold storage, decentralised protocols that resist central commands. Most citizens will sit somewhere in the middle, using a mix of bank accounts, custodial wallets, and perhaps a small self-custodied reserve.

The question then becomes: what guarantees, if any, should limit the switches available to those who operate custodial and public systems? A retail CBDC that permits instant blacklisting of individuals without review effectively rewrites due process. A stablecoin that can be frozen at the issuer's discretion introduces counterparty risk dressed as neutrality. A commercial bank with wide-ranging "terms of service" powers to close accounts for vague reasons can become an unofficial censor.

Law can in theory constrain these powers—judicial oversight, clear criteria, appeal mechanisms. The reality often lags. Emergency powers, once normalised, prove hard to roll back. Compliance departments rarely reward nuance. For risk-averse institutions, the easiest decision is to exit "troublesome" customers entirely: NGOs in geopolitically sensitive regions, independent media, sex workers, migrants. Policy endpoints proliferate, but they are informed more by risk scoring than democratic debate.

Programmable money systems amplify this trend because they reduce friction in enforcement. Freezing a card used to require individual action. Freezing a pattern of smart contract addresses can be done with one update to a blacklist. Geo-fencing certain wallets—say, all those with IP addresses in a sanctioned country—becomes a toggle rather than a project. The cost of extending control falls. The temptation to use it grows.

There are counter-moves. Some decentralised protocols enshrine governance rules that make blacklists difficult or impossible to apply without broad consensus. Others rely on zero-knowledge proofs to validate transactions without revealing identities, giving users plausible deniability. But these tools depend on adoption. A privacy-preserving wallet that few merchants accept will not serve most citizens.

We return to the motif of the switch. For a citizen to be more than a passive endpoint, they must know that switches exist, understand who operates them, and have some recourse when they are misused. Transparency about policy logic—what triggers a freeze, what behaviour flags an account, how to challenge an error—becomes as important as cryptographic soundness. Without it, programmable money risks turning into a black box where citizens are evaluated, rewarded, or punished by opaque algorithms.

There is a more optimistic reading. Properly designed, programmable money could distribute agency rather than concentrate it. Tax could be withheld automatically but reported with perfect clarity. Citizens could opt into savings schemes embedded in their wallets, with full visibility of terms. Local authorities could issue targeted rebates that citizens can redirect to causes of their choosing, turning fiscal flows into participatory budgeting. Self-custody skills could spread through education, much as literacy did, making financial autonomy less of a niche competence and more of a civic baseline.

Whether the technology realises this potential depends on whose problems it is built to solve. A system designed primarily to reduce administrative cost and tighten control will naturally treat citizens as endpoints to be managed. A system designed with rights in mind will impose constraints on itself—technical "speed bumps" on blacklisting, hard-coded privacy thresholds, multi-party approvals for invasive actions.

The unresolved tension sits where policy, code, and citizenship meet. As money becomes more programmable, each of us moves from being a background statistic in the economy to a node that code can address individually. The state, the bank, or the issuer looks at our wallet and can, in principle, decide: allow, delay, or deny.

The question is simple and uncomfortable. When the next crisis arrives and hands reach for the switch, will citizens stand merely as objects in someone else's control system, or as counterparts with recognised rights and credible means of exit?

Chapter 5
Institutions Enter the Arena

The boardroom was silent when the proposal landed on the table. It was February 2021, and MicroStrategy's directors had gathered at their headquarters in Tysons Corner, Virginia, to confront a question rarely seen in corporate minutes: should a publicly listed software firm place a material portion of its treasury reserves into Bitcoin? The spreadsheets were meticulous; the operational memos, less so. How would auditors treat irreversible wallet transfers? Who would hold the keys? What would it mean for quarterly volatility, for debt covenants, for reputational risk? The financial controller admitted he had never booked a digital bearer asset on an institutional ledger. Yet the balance sheet was melting under negative real yields, and inflation narratives echoed through every asset allocation discussion. The decision they took—one that reverberated across global markets—marked a moment when the esoteric edge of finance crossed the threshold into institutional consciousness.

This chapter begins at that threshold. For a decade, Bitcoin lived outside the formal walls of finance, a curiosity to some, an irritant to others. Its rails, culture, and incentives were built by individuals rather than institutions. But the moment large balance sheets began contemplating exposure—central bank treasuries testing pilot programmes, pension funds commissioning risk analyses, multinationals debating hedges—the nature of the conversation changed. The question was no longer *whether* Bitcoin could function as an asset. It was *how* it could fit into systems built for a different monetary species.

Institutional entry is not a story of adoption. It is a story of translation. Every time a treasury desk asks whether Bitcoin can behave like liquid collateral, every time a custodian designs a workflow to satisfy both cryptographers and regulators, every time an auditor searches for valuation standards in guidance that barely exists, the asset is reinterpreted. And reinterpretation is power. Institutions do not simply join an arena; they reshape it.

Maturity brings its own paradox. The very features that once defined Bitcoin—its indifference to intermediaries, its resistance to monetary dilution, its global neutrality—must be filtered through processes designed for liabilities, counterparty chains, and policy regimes. In this transition, the ideal of decentralisation encounters the gravitational pull of scale. Exchanges, custodians, and gatekeepers build the connective tissue between retail enthusiasm and institutional prudence. Yet every additional layer introduces a familiar dynamic: convenience purchased at the cost of centralisation.

Treasuries approach the field first, driven not by ideology but by arithmetic. When corporate finance teams model their cash positions under nominally safe instruments yielding less than inflation, an uncorrelated digital asset—however volatile—becomes a candidate for analysis. But operational friction remains real. How does a multinational reconcile global payment cycles with assets that settle every ten minutes? How do internal controls adapt to private keys that do not regenerate when lost? Institutions measure risk in basis points and compliance hours, not memes. Their calculus is methodical, and their hesitations reveal the collision between legacy infrastructure and cryptographic finality.

Investment funds follow with a different logic. They speak in mandates and benchmarks, in Sharpe ratios and liquidity screens. For them, the challenge is classification. Is Bitcoin a commodity, a currency, a speculative instrument, or a new category entirely? Asset managers need answers because regulation demands them. Yet global standards remain uneven, leaving institutional actors to build their own interpretive frameworks. A Swiss private bank may treat Bitcoin as digital gold; a U.S. pension fund may treat it as an alternative investment; a Singaporean sovereign entity may approach it as a long-term macro hedge. Each choice signals a narrative—and narratives move capital.

This tension between narrative and standardisation reaches its sharpest point in accounting. Balance sheets record what rules permit, not what markets believe. When fair value losses hit income statements while gains remain unrealised for reporting purposes, CFOs quickly sense that volatility is not merely a market property—it is a governance problem. The absence of harmonised global standards slows adoption more than any public scepticism. For institutions, uncertainty is a cost. Ambiguity is risk. And in the language of boards, risk must be justified.

Behind these questions sits a quieter, deeper force: the collective imagination of institutions. Risk committees do not respond to cryptography. They respond to stories. In the late 1970s, gold returned to institutional portfolios not because its metallurgy had changed, but because narratives of inflation, distrust of monetary authorities, and geopolitical flux made it symbolically potent. Bitcoin now competes in that same marketplace of stories. "Digital gold" shares the table with "speculative mania," "inflation hedge," and "uncorrelated macro asset." Directors debate not only spreadsheets but worldviews.

The chapter ahead explores this uneasy convergence. It examines why large balance sheets seek assets that lie outside the traditional financial web, even as their operational systems struggle to hold them. It considers how infrastructure providers—exchanges, custodians, market makers—mediate the ideals of decentralisation while nudging the ecosystem towards familiar hierarchies. It interrogates the lag between technological innovation and accounting standards, and how this lag shapes valuation, perception, and adoption curves. And it looks inside boardrooms, where narratives—sometimes disciplined, sometimes chaotic—frame the strategic entry points of institutional capital.

The stakes are not abstract. When institutions enter any arena, they bring scale, discipline, constraints, and expectations. They also bring political gravity. If Bitcoin is to coexist with the financial superstructure, that superstructure will demand interfaces, safeguards, and interpretations that alter the lived experience of the asset. Whether these adaptations enrich or dilute its core properties remains an open question.

What is clear is that institutions are no longer spectators. They are participants, shaping the ground while still learning its rules. The fault lines that emerge—between volatility and liquidity, decentralisation and convenience, narrative and governance—will define not only how Bitcoin is held, but what it becomes.

Treasuries, Corporates, and Funds: Balance sheets seek uncorrelated assets and liquid collateral. Treasury experiments face operational frictions

The email arrived at dawn on 11 August 2020. MicroStrategy, a mid-sized software company headquartered in Tysons Corner, Virginia, had disclosed a decision without precedent in U.S. corporate history: it had converted US$250 million of its treasury reserves into Bitcoin. The filing, timestamped and lodged with the Securities and Exchange Commission, landed like a stone in the placid waters of corporate finance. Treasury desks from London to Singapore read it twice. The action was real, the audit trail unambiguous, and the outcome immediate: a balance-sheet asset that could neither be diluted nor easily explained within familiar accounting categories. One director later remarked that the decision felt "both obvious and alien," a telling description of how institutional capital encounters the digital asset frontier.

The paradox was stark. A corporate treasury, an entity built on predictability, had opted for an asset famed for volatility. Yet the logic was not reckless. It was arithmetic. With policy rates pinned close to zero throughout mid-2020 and consumer inflation expectations rising, holding large pools of idle cash became a slow form of erosion. Treasury officers did what they always do: they compared risk to erosion. They modelled alternative assets. They tested liquidity conditions. They asked whether Bitcoin's uncorrelated return profile—so often debated in academic journals—might serve the same purpose that gold had served during inflationary episodes in the 1970s. A software company had forced a conservative discipline onto a radical asset.

This growing intersection between balance-sheet pragmatism and digital scarcity now defines one of the most consequential shifts in modern finance. Corporate treasuries, institutional funds, and sovereign entities have begun to treat Bitcoin not as a cultural artefact but as a line item competing for space among bonds, cash equivalents, and hedging instruments. Their motivations vary; their constraints do not. Every institutional actor steps into the arena with the same question: *can this asset behave in a way that my systems, my auditors, and my liquidity commitments can tolerate?* The answers reveal a tension between opportunity and friction.

Treasury management is built on a simple imperative: protect capital, preserve liquidity, and optimise yield. Show this principle at work and its implications become clearer. In March 2022, Block Inc., headquartered in San Francisco, disclosed holding over eight thousand bitcoins on its corporate balance sheet. The company presented the asset as long-term treasury support, recorded under impairment rules that forced downward revaluation while prohibiting upward adjustments unless realised through sale. Name the constraint: U.S. GAAP (as at 2022) classified Bitcoin as an indefinite-lived intangible asset, a treatment more suited to trademarks than liquid financial instruments. Explain its effect: treasurers contemplating even modest allocations had to accept the prospect of significant paper losses flowing through earnings without the relief of symmetrical gains.

Implication: institutional adoption slowed not because appetite was absent but because accounting rules froze volatility into income statements, hard-wiring prudential reluctance into the system.

Corporate treasuries face another obstacle: operational friction. Show it vividly. When Tesla announced its US$1.5 billion Bitcoin purchase in January 2021, traders focused on price impact; treasurers focused on custody. Where would keys reside? How would approval workflows map onto cryptographic signatures? What incident-response procedures were adequate for an asset with irreversible settlement? Name the mechanism: multi-signature custody, usually involving distributed key shards held across trusted counterparties. Explain the tension: multi-sig arrangements reduce operational risk but reintroduce a form of centralisation—legal agreements, control frameworks, dependency on service providers—that contradicts the asset's bearer ethos. Implication: corporate balance sheets tend to interpret decentralisation through the lens of operational risk, not ideology. What emerges is an asset shaped to fit institutional constraints rather than the purist's version of sovereignty.

Contrast these examples with a credible counter-example. El Salvador's sovereign Bitcoin purchases, formalised in September 2021 when the country adopted Bitcoin as legal tender, sidestepped traditional treasury frameworks. Custody arrangements were internalised; political leadership absorbed volatility rather than distributing responsibility across committees. But the limitation reveals itself quickly. Without the procedural checks, audited controls, and liquidity stress-testing that corporates and funds require, adoption becomes political theatre rather than institutional norm. Reconciling this illustrates a broader truth: institutions adopt when systems allow it, not when leaders declare it.

Funds approach the asset differently. Their behaviour is disciplined by mandates, liquidity screens, and risk metrics visible on quarterly reports. Show this dynamic. In October 2021, ProShares launched the first U.S. Bitcoin futures exchange-traded fund (ETF) under ticker BITO. Its structure used regulated CME Bitcoin futures rather than spot holdings, allowing compliance with the Investment Company Act of 1940. Name the issue: futures roll costs. Explain: the fund incurred persistent negative carry whenever the futures curve was in contango, creating tracking deviations from spot Bitcoin. Implication: although the ETF absorbed billions in flows within days, many institutional allocators remained on the sidelines because the instrument's performance diverged from the underlying asset. It was a bridge, but a flawed bridge.

Contrast that with a second institutional example. In January 2024, the U.S. Securities and Exchange Commission approved a suite of spot Bitcoin ETFs, allowing issuers such as BlackRock and Fidelity to hold actual Bitcoin on behalf of fund investors. The custodial arrangements were concentrated: Coinbase, a single NASDAQ-listed exchange, provided custody for most issuers. The visible behaviour—the concentration of trillions of potential future flows through one custodial channel—exposed a structural weakness. Bitcoin, designed as a decentralised network, had entered the institutional sphere through an architecture that recentralised risk. The implication is not doom but a shift: systemic significance now depends less on protocol resilience and more on operational chokepoints created by market structure.

The institutional search for uncorrelated assets is old, but Bitcoin alters the terms of the search. A pension fund in Rotterdam or Toronto cannot simply decide that Bitcoin is "uncorrelated." It must measure correlation over time horizons, examine liquidity during stress periods, and model liquidation pathways for redemption cycles. Correlations that appear low in calm markets may spike under macro stress. Bitcoin's price collapse in March 2020, when it fell over 40 percent in a single day amid global liquidity panic, demonstrates this. Yet the recovery that followed—one of the fastest of any major asset—suggests a more nuanced pattern: Bitcoin behaves like a high-beta macro asset during liquidity shocks but reverts to idiosyncratic drivers once conditions normalise. Institutions measure these behaviours not with sentiment but with daily covariance matrices, stress scenarios, and liquidity buckets. This measurement discipline acts as a sieve through which Bitcoin must pass.

The motif that threads through the institutional experience is friction: frictions of accounting, custody, liquidity, governance, and narrative. Each friction reveals a point where a decentralised asset must pass through a centralised system. Consider liquidity. Bitcoin trades continuously, settles irreversibly within minutes, and clears without counterparties. Yet a corporate cash-flow cycle operates on banking hours, approval chains, and reconciliations that assume reversibility. Show the collision: a treasury office managing payroll cannot rely on an asset whose settlement finality is immediate and unforgiving. Name the adaptation: derivative overlays, structured redemption windows, and blended portfolios that pair Bitcoin exposure with liquid hedges. Explain the cost: the more institutions normalise Bitcoin, the more they build layers around it to make it resemble traditional instruments. Implication: institutional adoption tends to domesticate the asset.

Another friction sits in collateral. Some hedge funds now post Bitcoin as collateral for derivatives or borrowing arrangements, but only under strict valuation haircuts. In 2023, several prime brokers accepted Bitcoin at haircuts of 30 percent or more. The behaviour, visible in term sheets, shows that institutions treat Bitcoin as high-volatility collateral requiring conservative buffers. Name the rationale: daily price swings. Explain the consequence: capital efficiency drops. Implication: until volatility declines materially or pricing frameworks mature, Bitcoin will remain a marginal collateral asset for many funds, limiting its integration into global liquidity cycles.

Yet friction can be productive. It forces precision. It compels institutions to confront what Bitcoin is, not what narratives claim. Treasury advisers who once dismissed the asset now ask technical questions about multi-party computation, cold-storage segregation, and key-rotation schedules. They compare settlement finality with SWIFT lead times. They evaluate how Bitcoin behaves during central-bank tightening cycles. These behaviours mark the progress of institutional literacy.

But institutional interest also carries risk. When a limited number of custodians control access for the largest pools of capital, concentration risk rises. When narratives of inflation hedging or digital gold spread through boardrooms without corresponding understanding of market structure, expectations can outrun capacity. And when balance sheets grow comfortable with exposure but remain uncomfortable with self-custody, the ecosystem tilts towards recentralisation.

The unresolved tension sits here: can an asset designed to remove intermediaries thrive inside institutions built on intermediaries? The answer will depend on whether institutions adapt their frameworks or reshape the asset to fit those frameworks. Treasuries, corporates, and funds now stand at that fork. Their next decisions—about custody, collateral, liquidity, and governance—will reveal whether institutional adoption becomes a translation or a transformation.

Exchanges, Custodians, and Gatekeepers

On the evening of 8 November 2022 in Nassau, customers of FTX still saw green numbers on their screens. Bitcoin balances, dollar balances, neatly listed altcoins—the interface gave no hint that the exchange's internal wallets were nearly empty. Within hours, withdrawals halted. By 11 November, FTX had filed for bankruptcy in Delaware. Court documents later suggested that billions of dollars of customer assets were missing. An exchange that marketed itself as a safer, more sophisticated gateway to crypto had imploded in a fashion depressingly familiar to traditional finance veterans: poor controls, hidden leverage, commingled funds. A decentralised asset had been recentralised inside a black box. When the box broke, Bitcoin's rules did not fail. The market structure around it did.

The screens looked reassuringly normal. That was the point. For most users, FTX *was* Bitcoin. It was where they bought, sold, and stored it. The chain's transparent ledger and self-custody ideals mattered little compared with the ease of a login and a password reset link. This is the paradox at the core of our subject: networks designed to reduce reliance on intermediaries end up funnelling risk through a small set of intermediaries because most participants prefer convenience. Exchanges, custodians, and other gatekeepers become the practical face of a protocol that was supposed to have no face at all.

The quiet motif here is the doorway. Whoever controls the doorway to a system can shape what enters, what leaves, and who stands in the queue. The more people who use the same doorway, the more power accrues to whoever guards it.

Centralised exchanges emerged first as simple matching engines with web front-ends. Mt. Gox in Tokyo, active from 2010 until its collapse in 2014, handled an estimated 70 percent of global Bitcoin trading at its peak. When Mt. Gox "lost" around 850,000 bitcoins due to theft and mismanagement, it demonstrated a harsh truth: users had not owned coins; they had owned claims on coins. The behaviour—customers refreshing withdrawal pages that never cleared—revealed the structural risk of custodial concentration. One doorway for most of the world's flow. One lock. One failure.

Market structure evolved but did not abandon the basic model. Major exchanges like Binance, Coinbase, and Kraken offer order books, custody, derivatives, staking, yield products, and fiat on-ramps in a single vertically integrated stack. For many participants, these platforms are indistinguishable from full-service banks, except that deposits are not insured to the same degree and governance can be opaque. Order execution, collateral management, lending, and proprietary trading often occur within the same corporate perimeter. This co-location of activities mirrors the universal bank model that post-crisis regulation tried to separate. It increases convenience. It also increases internal conflicts of interest.

Show how this mediates ideals. Bitcoin's credible neutrality depends on equal access to the network: anyone can broadcast a transaction, anyone can verify one. Centralised exchanges impose new rules: know-your-customer checks, geographical blocks, delisting of addresses, suspensions at the request of authorities. Coinbase's decision in 2022 to block accounts belonging to sanctioned Russian individuals was legal and arguably prudent. Yet it also underscored that exchange balances do not enjoy the protocol's censorship-resistance. The implication is straightforward: once holdings are re-intermediated, account access becomes a policy variable, not a protocol guarantee. The doorway obeys law, not code.

Custody crystallises this dynamic. Institutional investors rarely self-custody. They rely on regulated custodians with insurance policies, SOC 2 reports, and segregation of duties. Firms like Coinbase Custody, Fidelity Digital Assets, and various specialist providers hold keys in cold storage or use multi-party computation schemes. This professionalisation solves real problems: it reduces key-loss risk, enables institutional access, and satisfies regulators. But it also recentralises control. When a handful of custodians hold assets on behalf of pension funds, ETFs, and corporates, those entities become systemic chokepoints. A software bug, regulatory freeze, or legal judgement at the custodian level can immobilise large fractions of circulating supply. The asset is decentralised. Its possession is not.

The concentration became more visible as spot Bitcoin ETFs began to launch in large jurisdictions. Several issuers selected the same few custodians to store underlying coins. The behaviour is rational—scale, brand, and regulatory licences matter. Yet the implication is uncomfortable: market structure funnels much of the institutional Bitcoin supply through two or three vaults. The mythology of "distributed coins in a million wallets" coexists with a reality of "a few massive omnibus accounts and thousands of beneficial owners recorded in databases". The risk profile starts to resemble traditional securities custody, with familiar benefits and familiar vulnerabilities.

Exchanges also act as de facto regulators through listing decisions. When Coinbase lists a new asset, liquidity usually surges and prices often spike. When Binance delists a coin, liquidity can evaporate overnight. These choices determine which projects gain access to global capital and which remain marginal. They also reflect, implicitly, each platform's interpretation of regulatory risk. Tokens that resemble securities may be excluded from certain markets; privacy coins may be delisted due to anti-money-laundering concerns. The ideals of permissionless innovation collide with gatekeeping. Developers who can deploy code to a public blockchain with no one's approval still find that, without listings, their tokens have little practical reach. The doorway decides whose voices carry.

Market makers deepen these dynamics. On most order-book exchanges, a small number of algorithmic firms provide the majority of liquidity. They quote bids and offers, arbitrage price differences across venues, and, in some cases, operate in close partnership with the exchanges themselves. The behaviour can be constructive—tighter spreads, better execution. It can also amplify fragility. When volatility spikes, market makers widen spreads or pull quotes. During the March 2020 "Black Thursday" crash, several exchanges saw cascading liquidations as derivatives positions blew out and liquidity vanished. The same pipes that channelled inflows during bull markets transmitted forced selling during stress. Again, the protocol did not fail; the market structure did, briefly.

Against this backdrop, decentralised exchanges (DEXs) emerged as a counter-example. Platforms like Uniswap, launched in 2018 on Ethereum, allow users to trade directly from self-custodied wallets using automated market maker algorithms. There is no central order book. Liquidity comes from pools of tokens deposited by users in exchange for fees. The model reduces custody risk: users do not transfer coins to a central account. It also reduces gatekeeping: anyone can create a trading pair by depositing assets into a new pool.

Yet the DEX model introduces its own gatekeepers and frictions. Front-end websites that ordinary users rely on can be geo-blocked or taken down. Liquidity often depends on stablecoins issued by centralised entities. Price feeds rely on oracles. Miners and validators can reorder transactions to extract "maximum extractable value" (MEV), front-running trades and eroding user returns. Governance tokens confer control over protocol parameters to a small group of large holders. The doorways have changed shape. They have not disappeared.

Decentralised and centralised venues also interact in complex ways. Arbitrageurs keep prices aligned across them. When centralised exchanges delist an asset, DEXs may remain open, but liquidity can fragment and spreads widen. When centralised venues halt withdrawals, DEX prices can detach from the broader market because arbitrage flows stall. The result is a layered market where failures in one segment propagate through others. A decentralised base does not guarantee a stable superstructure.

Gatekeeping also operates at the level of infrastructure. Banking relationships determine which exchanges can offer fiat on-ramps. When major U.S. banks in 2023 reduced or severed relationships with certain crypto firms after high-profile failures, those exchanges saw fiat volumes drop. Customers could no longer move dollars in and out as easily. This did not reflect protocol risk so much as reputational contagion. Yet for users, the effect was identical: an asset that had traded seamlessly now sat behind a higher barrier. The doorway narrowed.

Regulators face their own paradox. They want to reduce systemic risk and protect consumers, which pushes them to favour well-capitalised, supervised exchanges and custodians. But privileging a small set of players hardens their dominance. When a regulator signals that "only institutions meeting these standards may operate", it may, unintentionally, crown gatekeepers. This is not unique to crypto; banking regulation has long displayed similar dynamics. The difference is that, in the Bitcoin context, this concentration jars with the founding ethos.

There are attempts to reconcile these tensions. Some custody providers experiment with models where clients retain a key shard, ensuring that assets cannot move without client participation. Some exchanges segregate client funds on-chain, providing proof-of-reserves attestations that allow users to verify holdings. After FTX's collapse, several platforms published Merkle-tree based proofs of liabilities and associated on-chain addresses. These steps push market structure closer to the transparency of the underlying protocol. But they remain voluntary, uneven, and technically daunting for many users to interpret.

Meanwhile, "not your keys, not your coins" has become a rallying cry encouraging self-custody. Hardware wallet sales spiked after each major exchange failure. Behaviour shifted, at least temporarily, towards more sovereign practices. Yet most new entrants still begin their journey through centralised platforms. For them, the exchange is the brand they recognise, the app they use daily. The blockchain remains abstract until something breaks.

The doorway motif returns. Bitcoin's ledger is open to all. But the effective experience of Bitcoin for the majority is mediated by a handful of doorways: a few exchanges, a few custodians, a few indexing services, a few data providers. Those entities decide which assets are visible, which features are exposed, which jurisdictions are served, and which behaviours trigger friction.

The unresolved tension is climate rather than weather. As Bitcoin and similar assets mature, will market structure converge on a model that preserves meaningful exit to self-custody and diverse access routes, or will convenience and regulation push the ecosystem towards a small number of tightly controlled gateways? Put differently: when the next generation of users arrive and reach for the handle, whose doorway will they find—and what, precisely, will it lead to?

Accounting, Valuation, and Signals

On 8 February 2021 in California, Tesla announced in an SEC filing that it had purchased $1.5 billion of bitcoin. Within minutes, headlines ricocheted across global markets. Bitcoin's price surged. Tesla's own shares jumped before fading. Yet when Tesla later reported quarterly results, the company disclosed an impairment: under U.S. GAAP, crypto holdings were classified as indefinite-lived intangible assets. Prices could move up and down intraday, but accounting only recognised downward movements. Gains remained invisible unless Tesla sold. Losses were immediate. A balance-sheet signal that had electrified markets was dampened by rules written for older technologies. The ledger of the protocol moved swiftly. The ledger of corporate accounting moved slowly.

The tension was not about volatility alone. It was about meaning. Investors saw one number—the fair market value of Tesla's holdings, refreshed tick by tick. Accountants reported another—the historical cost minus any impairments. Two ledgers, two truths, converging only at the moment of sale. By the end of 2021, analysts could estimate Tesla's unrealised gains with reasonable precision, but the financial statements embedded none of that appreciation. The signal investors craved was muted by the standards they relied upon. Five words capture the paradox: the numbers lag reality.

The motif is the shadow. Every valuation method casts one: a silhouette of economic truth shaped by the direction of illumination. When standards lag innovation, shadows grow long, and the outlines matter more than the detail beneath.

Standards bodies recognised the gap. Accounting rules in the United States had evolved for software licences, trademarks, and goodwill—assets with intangible characteristics but not with continuously observable market prices. The FASB's decision in 2023 to adopt fair-value accounting for certain crypto assets marked a turning point. Under the new framework, firms could finally report gains and losses symmetrically. This was a visible behaviour: corporates began disclosing their holdings in greater detail, reflecting rising comfort with transparent mark-to-market presentation. The implication was straightforward: when economic reality becomes easier to express, adoption becomes easier to justify.

The history of financial reporting shows the same rhythm across earlier innovations. In London in 1971, when the first modern financial futures contracts gained traction on U.S. exchanges, British corporates faced an unfamiliar problem:

how to account for instruments whose value fluctuated daily and whose payoff profiles were nonlinear. The early standards lagged practice, creating mismatches where firms hedged exposures effectively but produced volatile reported results because hedges and underlying items were not recognised consistently. Practice led. Standards followed. With Bitcoin and other digital assets, the cycle repeats with different actors and higher public scrutiny.

A second example comes from corporate treasuries during the 1990s tech boom. Companies such as Microsoft and Apple accumulated large cash piles invested in short-term instruments. Mark-to-market rules under FAS 115, introduced in 1993, forced firms to classify securities as trading, available-for-sale, or held-to-maturity. The classification determined whether unrealised gains and losses flowed through profit and loss or through other comprehensive income. The behaviour to note is the strategic placement of securities by treasurers to manage earnings volatility. This reveals a consistent truth: reporting choices shape external interpretations as much as underlying performance.

Bitcoin poses its own twist. Unlike securities with explicit contractual cash flows, Bitcoin has no coupon, dividend, or maturity date. Its valuation is purely market-driven. Mark-to-market treatment therefore binds the balance sheet directly to a volatile market narrative. The implications are far from trivial. For firms with monthly or quarterly reporting cycles, sharp interim price swings become earnings swings. The shadow grows long again.

Corporate boards recognise this interplay. Risk committees weigh not only the economic rationale for holding Bitcoin—hedging, liquidity management, collateral flexibility—but also the accounting impact. A company that adds a small Bitcoin allocation may find that the volatility of reported earnings overwhelms the narrative of prudent diversification. In such cases, boards often choose delay, not rejection. They wait for clearer measurement standards, lower operational friction, or a demonstration effect from peers. Adoption curves flatten not because the asset lacks merit, but because the reporting noise contaminates the signal.

Two more examples illustrate the potency of that signal. In 2020, MicroStrategy adopted Bitcoin as a treasury reserve asset. Its CEO, Michael Saylor, announced the decision in August of that year. The firm's disclosures showed an accumulation that grew to billions of dollars. Yet under then-current accounting standards, rising prices did not lift reported earnings; falling prices did depress them. The company's share price became tightly correlated with Bitcoin's, sometimes overshadowing its underlying software business. The implication was clear: valuation treatment can reframe a company itself, transforming its perceived identity from a software firm to a Bitcoin proxy.

By contrast, when the Swiss city of Zug launched a pilot in 2016 allowing residents to pay certain administrative fees in Bitcoin, the accounting footprint told a different story. Fees were converted immediately into Swiss francs. Bitcoin served as a payment rail, not a balance-sheet asset. The volatility risk vanished; the reporting burden remained minimal. The behaviour—instant conversion—revealed a pathway for institutional experimentation without long-term valuation exposure. It also highlighted a recurring limitation: many institutions use crypto rails but avoid crypto exposure. The rail is embraced, the asset avoided.

A credible counter-example lies in entities that maintain Bitcoin balances for extended periods without mark-to-market disclosure. Certain foundations and non-profits, particularly in the early 2010s, accepted donations in Bitcoin but recorded them at the fiat value on the day of receipt. If the value rose dramatically, the uplift often appeared only when assets were sold. This practice under-reported economic resources and distorted donor perceptions. Yet these organisations operated with far less regulatory scrutiny and far simpler financial statements. The limitation, then, is not that accounting standards inevitably hinder innovation, but that their absence or looseness can also obscure truth. Reconciling this teaches a simple lesson: standards exist to illuminate, but when ill-suited, they generate more shadow than light.

The dynamics of valuation also affect macro-scale adoption. Large asset managers must follow strict mandates determining what they can hold. If Bitcoin is classified as a commodity, certain funds can include it. If it is treated as an intangible, others cannot. As of 2024, regulatory interpretations in the United States, Europe, and Asia differ. These divergences filter directly into institutional demand. The behaviour is visible: some exchange-traded products attract billions within months; others languish with thin volume. Categorisation changes capital.

Signals operate beyond balance sheets. Mark-to-market valuation influences corporate decision-making itself. A firm that holds Bitcoin may decide against using it as operational collateral if the volatility profile threatens covenants or internal risk limits. A treasurer may reduce exposure ahead of a quarter-end reporting window to avoid earnings surprises. Such decisions create feedback loops. When many firms behave similarly, Bitcoin's volatility can increase around reporting dates. The market begins to anticipate these flows. The shadow moves with expectation, not just with fundamentals.

Auditors play a pivotal role. Their comfort determines whether firms adopt more sophisticated custody arrangements, such as multi-signature wallets or MPC-based key distribution. Early in the adoption cycle, some audit firms resisted signing off on these structures due to unfamiliarity. As expertise grew, auditors began to require more rigorous segregation of duties, clearer key-management processes, and enhanced third-party attestations. This behaviour shapes practice: when audit requirements stiffen, firms invest in robust operational controls. The implication is encouraging. As knowledge diffuses, institutions become more competent stewards of digital assets.

A persistent tension lies in the difference between measurement and meaning. Market price is a measurement. Narrative is meaning. In financial reporting, the two are often conflated. A rising Bitcoin price can signal investor confidence, inflation hedging, speculative mania, or technological optimism depending on context. When prices fall, interpretations swing to fear, exhaustion, or regulatory concern. Boards interpret these movements differently from analysts. Accountants interpret them differently again. The valuation number remains the same; the stories diverge.

Mark-to-market also produces path dependence. Early adopters whose holdings rose sharply during bull markets can weather subsequent drawdowns without impairing capital. Later entrants who buy near peaks bear impairments quickly. Boards remember these experiences. A CFO who lived through a bruising impairment cycle will likely approach future digital asset exposures with caution. Time, entry point, and reporting rules entwine.

Standard-setters attempt to reduce this path dependence by emphasising disclosure. Detailed notes on custody arrangements, valuation methodologies, and fair-value hierarchy levels provide context beyond the numbers. These disclosures help investors distinguish between firms that actively manage their exposure and those that allow it to drift. Yet disclosure can only go so far. The headline numbers dominate: impairments, fair-value gains, unrealised losses. Signals compress complexity into a single line item.

A deeper tension sits beneath all this. Bitcoin was designed as a self-verifying ledger with no need for external trust.

Institutions operate on trusted systems of verification—audits, standards, legal frameworks. When institutions enter, they bring their norms with them. The result is an overlap of two systems: one that marks truth by consensus of code, and one that marks truth by consensus of standards. When those consensuses diverge—even subtly—interpretation becomes delicate. The shadow of one ledger falls across the other.

Some firms experiment with hybrid approaches. They maintain a small operational Bitcoin balance for settlement but hedge price exposure through derivatives. They use internal dashboards showing both mark-to-market and long-term cost bases. They simulate impairment scenarios under extreme volatility. These behaviours suggest that institutions do not reject Bitcoin; they adapt it to existing frameworks. Yet such adaptations influence perception. Bitcoin becomes another line item in a risk-managed portfolio, its ideological edges softened for compliance.

The quiet motif returns: the shadow that valuation casts. Institutions operate in that shadow because they must. Standards ensure comparability, predictability, and legal certainty. Innovation challenges these structures by moving faster than they can adjust. The shadow is not failure. It is lag.

A final dilemma remains. If Bitcoin continues to mature, will accounting standards converge on a stable, globally recognised framework that reflects its economic properties with precision, or will divergent regional approaches fragment adoption and complicate cross-border holdings? Put differently: when future leaders assess digital assets, will they peer at the number itself—or at the shadow it casts?

Narratives that Move Boards

On 9 February 2021, in a glass-walled boardroom in Palo Alto, Tesla's directors reviewed the consequences of the decision they had taken just weeks earlier: to allocate US$1.5 billion of

corporate cash to Bitcoin. The numbers were extraordinary. In a matter of days, the mark-to-market gain on the position had exceeded the company's entire 2020 net profit. One director turned to the CFO and asked a deceptively simple question: "What story are we telling our shareholders now?" The spreadsheets showed volatility, correlations, liquidity profiles. The conversation circled something less tangible: Tesla had ceased to be just an electric car company. It had become, in part, a macro bet. A narrative shift had occurred, and the board knew it.
Risk committees like to imagine themselves as strongholds of quantification. They measure VaR, run stress tests, and label scenarios with tidy probabilities. Yet when an asset such as Bitcoin enters the agenda, the formal tools are often a beat behind the conversation. Directors ask: *Is this a speculative punt? A hedge against inflation? A strategic reserve like digital gold? A signal of innovation to customers and staff?* Each description carries different implications for responsibility and time horizon. Each gives different cover if things go badly. The numbers matter. The story decides.

A quiet motif runs through these rooms: the question on the slide. Not the chart or the table, but the sentence that frames them. Is Bitcoin "portfolio insurance", "optionality", or "speculative surplus"? Boards do not answer data. They answer that sentence.

The first narrative, usually the loudest, is speculation. Bitcoin is framed as a high-beta, momentum-driven asset that might turbocharge returns but could just as easily scorch them. Show how this plays out. At a hedge fund's investment committee in London in late 2020, a portfolio manager pitches a 2 per cent Bitcoin allocation as "asymmetric upside". He points to past cycles: 80 per cent drawdowns followed by multi-hundred per cent rallies. He has back-tested a strategy: buy when momentum crosses a threshold; cap exposure; rebalance quarterly. The language is tactical: "entry points", "position sizing", "stop-loss discipline". Directors probe operational details but accept the underlying frame: this is a trade, not a statement. If it fails, it joins the graveyard of other trades. The time horizon is short. Memory is forgiving.

The implication of this speculative framing is subtle. It allows boards to approve exposure without rethinking their worldview. Bitcoin is not a challenge to monetary architecture; it is volatile stuff to be handled with tongs. That minimises institutional discomfort but also caps depth of engagement. Treasury policies remain unchanged. Risk appetites stay familiar. The asset is quarantined in a mental bucket labelled "other".

The second narrative, more ambitious and contentious, is inflation hedging. Here, Bitcoin is presented as an antidote to monetary expansion and negative real yields. The story runs through history: the abandonment of the gold standard, the erosion of purchasing power, the limited supply of 21 million coins coded into Bitcoin's protocol. Show it concretely. In 2020, amid extraordinary fiscal and monetary interventions during the pandemic, asset managers such as Ruffer in London disclosed significant Bitcoin positions, explicitly citing a desire to hedge "monetary debasement" risk. Behaviour followed story: rather than a tactical trade, the allocation was described as a macro hedge expected to play out over years.

Boards confronting this narrative face a heavier burden. They must form a view not only on Bitcoin but on central banks, sovereign debt sustainability, and the trajectory of inflation. The risk committee becomes an arena for competing macro stories. One director cites the 1970s: oil shocks, stagflation, gold's meteoric rise. Another points to Japan's multi-decade low-rate environment as a counter-example: massive balance sheets, yet subdued inflation. A third notes that Bitcoin is less than two decades old and has never experienced a full tightening cycle until recently. The implication is that the "digital inflation hedge" story rests on thin historical soil.

Real behaviour reveals the difficulty. During the 2021–2022 period of rising inflation and rate hikes, Bitcoin did not reliably move opposite to inflation or central bank rhetoric. At times it traded more like a high-growth technology stock, selling off as real yields rose. This challenged the simplicity of the hedge story. Boards that had adopted an inflation-hedging narrative found themselves explaining why the "hedge" drew down alongside risk assets. The story had to be refined: Bitcoin as a long-run hedge against extreme monetary outcomes rather than a short-run refuge from CPI surprises. The motif returns. The question on the slide changed from "Does Bitcoin hedge inflation?" to "Which inflation scenario are we actually hedging?"

The third narrative, and the one with the deepest institutional resonance, is digital gold. Here Bitcoin is cast not as a currency or a hedge against next quarter's CPI print, but as an emergent store of value akin to gold—scarce, supranational, and uncorrelated with traditional credit assets over long horizons. The metaphor does heavy lifting. Directors understand gold. Central banks hold it. Insurance companies model it. A gold analogy places Bitcoin in a conceptual lineage that feels familiar.

Show how this narrative operates. An investment committee at a European family office in 2021 hears a proposal to reallocate a small portion of its 5 per cent gold allocation into Bitcoin over a ten-year horizon. The adviser presents data: long-term gold returns versus inflation, correlations with equities and bonds, Bitcoin's supply schedule versus historical gold mining output. The story is evolutionary: from physical scarcity to digital scarcity. The behaviour this framing invites is distinct. Allocation sizes are modest. Turnover is low. The asset is placed in the "strategic reserve" bucket, not the "tactical opportunity" one.

Yet the digital gold story faces a credible counter-example: gold itself. When geopolitical stress spikes—Russia's invasion of Ukraine in early 2022, for instance—gold tends to rally as a safe haven. Bitcoin, by contrast, has often fallen alongside risk assets in the initial shock. The behaviour suggests that, at least for now, markets still treat Bitcoin as a high-risk asset, not as an uncorrelated store of value. Boards see this. Some treat the discrepancy as evidence that the digital gold narrative is aspirational. Others treat it as disqualifying. Reconciliation requires nuance: Bitcoin may be on a path towards store-of-value status, but its current profile still reflects speculative and macro sensitivities.

That nuance shows up in practice. A pension fund in Canada might conclude that regulatory, reputational, and volatility constraints make direct allocation impossible, yet still allow a venture sleeve to invest in Bitcoin infrastructure. The narrative becomes "innovation optionality" rather than "digital gold". The same board, revisiting the question five years later, might update its story if liquidity deepens, volatility falls, and regulatory frameworks stabilise. Narratives evolve, not just positions.

Examples beyond Bitcoin help anchor this pattern. When gold was reintroduced into institutional portfolios after the collapse of Bretton Woods, boards did not adopt it overnight. They debated whether it was a barbarous relic, a hedge, or a geopolitical insurance policy. In the early 2000s, inflation-linked bonds faced similar narrative battles: were they a niche instrument or a core asset class for liability-driven investment? In both cases, the eventual outcome depended less on the assets' intrinsic properties—these changed slowly—than on the stories that gained traction among influential allocators.

Risk committees are particularly sensitive to narrative because narrative governs blame. If a board approves Bitcoin under a "speculation" frame and the trade fails, the loss is regrettable but contained. If it approves under a "store of value" frame and the asset collapses during a crisis, the loss looks like a category error. Directors fear that. They ask: *What will we say in the letter to shareholders if this halves?* That question shapes sizing, timing, counterparties, even whether the proposal reaches the agenda at all.

Signals from peers feed these stories. When a company like MicroStrategy embraces Bitcoin aggressively and sees its share price respond, other boards pay attention—not because they envy the bravado, but because markets have reacted. When insurers such as MassMutual in the United States announced in December 2020 that they had purchased US$100 million of Bitcoin for their general account, the amount was tiny relative to their balance sheet. The narrative impact was not. It signalled that a deeply conservative institution had found a story it could live with: a modest, long-horizon allocation framed as diversification rather than speculation. Risk committees at other insurers could point to that precedent when justifying their own explorations.

The motif of the question on the slide can be seen in the memos that precede board discussions. Internal documents often begin not with a recommendation, but with a framing line: "This paper considers whether and how Bitcoin might play a strategic role in our asset allocation over a ten-year horizon." Or: "This note examines the suitability of Bitcoin as a tactical inflation hedge in the current macro environment." These sentences do more than introduce. They bound the debate. They define what counts as success. They influence which data is deemed relevant.

There is also a narrative of omission: the story that keeps Bitcoin out of the room. In many institutions, the default frame is "career risk". Senior executives may personally believe that digital assets will matter, yet hesitate to champion them because the downside of being wrong is greater than the upside of being early. Behaviour betrays this: polite postponement, repeated "we'll revisit once regulation clarifies", delegating the topic to exploratory committees without capital authority. This too is a story: that prudence consists in waiting until the asset is uncontroversial. It is not irrational. It is path dependent.

Boards also grapple with internal narrative pluralism. A chief technology officer may view Bitcoin as an infrastructure innovation; a chief risk officer, as an unmodelled tail-risk factor; a chief marketing officer, as a brand alignment opportunity in crypto-friendly segments. In a long evening meeting, these perspectives clash. The CIO tries to synthesise: perhaps a pilot project, perhaps a tiny allocation, perhaps a "watching brief". What emerges from these negotiations is not the most accurate view of Bitcoin, but the most acceptable story for that specific institution at that specific moment.

Two forces then determine adoption curves. The first is exogenous: regulation, market infrastructure, accounting standards. The second is narrative fitness: the degree to which a story about Bitcoin can plug into an organisation's existing mental models without breaking them. A bank steeped in Basel capital ratios will find comfort in a framing that emphasises liquidity, haircuts, and collateral roles. A tech company will find comfort in an "innovation" narrative. A university endowment, charged with intergenerational stewardship, will be drawn to long-horizon, low-probability, high-impact stories.

The unresolved tension is not whether one narrative is "true". Bitcoin can be, and often is, simultaneously a vehicle for speculation, a candidate hedge against certain macro paths, and an aspirant digital store of value. The tension lies in which of these stories boards choose to underwrite with institutional capital, and at what scale. The choice will not be made by the most elegant model, but by the story that directors believe they can defend—in the minutes, in the press release, and, most of all, in front of their future selves when they reread today's decisions with the benefit of hindsight.

Chapter 6
The Regulation Wars

In October 2022, a quiet drama unfolded behind a closed door in Brussels. A technical working group—lawyers, code auditors, central bankers—was attempting to finalise a definition of "custody" under the EU's new Markets in Crypto-Assets Regulation. The question looked surgical: *when does a software wallet cross the line from tool to regulated service?* Yet as the arguments rolled through the room, it became clear the stakes were far larger. A single phrase could determine whether a handful of developers became financial intermediaries overnight, or whether billions in digital assets could flow through an unlicensed seam in the system. One participant, exasperated, tapped the table and said: "We are trying to pin down a moving target with a ruler that keeps changing shape." The line lingered. It captured the central tension of this chapter: the world's legal systems are attempting to govern a monetary technology that evolves faster than their concepts.

The paradox sits in plain view. States rely on definitions—"issuer", "transfer", "client", "finality"—to enforce financial rules. Blockchains rely on consensus, which is agnostic to those definitions. When a protocol upgrade rolls out or a new wallet design obviates an old compliance mechanism, the legal perimeter wobbles. Rapid change meets slow text. The result is a widening seam in which regulators fear systemic risk and innovators fear regulatory overreach. Both sides insist they are protecting the system's integrity. Both are partly right.

A motif threads through this terrain: the border post. Every financial system erects them—points where identity, legality, and accountability must be shown. Some are gates staffed by supervisors. Some are invisible lines in code. Some, increasingly, move with the network itself. The fights are never only about money. They are about who owns the border post, who gets to stand at it, and who can walk through uninspected.

This chapter enters that contested ground. The regulatory wars are not an ideological showdown between libertarian engineers and bureaucratic traditionalists. They are a series of structural collisions between two models of order. One is built on principles and precedent; the other, on protocols and peer-to-peer rules. In the UK and EU, where most examples in this chapter sit, the regulatory DNA leans towards proportionality, risk-based approaches, and functional definitions. But even there, the seams show. When law meets code, neither emerges unchanged.

The first set of collisions arises from the conceptual architecture of regulation itself. Principle-based systems attempt to articulate broad duties—act with integrity, safeguard assets, prevent illicit finance—and trust supervised firms to interpret them responsibly. Rule-based systems enumerate obligations with granular precision. Both approaches strain when technology mutates too quickly for doctrine to keep pace. The UK's reliance on high-level tests offers flexibility but creates ambiguity: is a validator providing a regulated service? Does a DeFi interface "arrange" a transaction? Meanwhile, the EU's more detailed checklists promise clarity but risk obsolescence when protocols shift. A regulation drafted around fixed custodial flows struggles when self-custody tools automate away intermediaries. The border post moves, but the legal map does not.

The next frontier is the regulatory perimeter itself: the line that defines who falls under supervision and why. Licences are not just authorisations—they are classifications. They determine which activities are trusted, which are tolerated, and which are punished. In traditional finance, custody, brokerage, and issuance are well understood. In crypto, these roles blur. A wallet can be a vault, a router, or a sovereign tool of personal finance. A smart contract can operate as a clearinghouse without personnel. A protocol upgrade can change risk profiles overnight. Regulators, facing this shifting terrain, default to functional triggers: holding customer assets, controlling private keys, matching orders, providing ongoing access. Yet each trigger has blind spots. A hardware wallet that never touches a private key might escape oversight, even if its firmware updates silently shape user security. A custodial exchange may comply perfectly, yet funnel user funds into opaque rehypothecation practices, as the collapse of FTX in November 2022 revealed.

Operational frictions reinforce these uncertainties. Treasury teams experimenting with digital assets discover that regulatory uncertainty is not a theoretical problem but a daily operational one. Compliance officers ask whether a transfer to a protocol located "everywhere and nowhere" constitutes dealing with an unlicensed entity. Payment flows stall as legal teams dissect whether a wrapped token is a derivative. Even simple questions—who is the counterparty? where does settlement occur?—produce more heat than clarity. The border post flickers.

But the most profound shift—one that forces regulators to grapple with code as a regulatory substrate—comes from compliance itself becoming a matter of architecture. Travel-rule requirements demand metadata: who is sending what to whom. But blockchains, by design, broadcast transactions pseudonymously, not identities. The result is a fork in design paths. One path embeds surveillance-heavy controls: wallet attestation systems, transfer screening, blacklists baked into infrastructure. The other path explores privacy-preserving compliance using zero-knowledge proofs, selective disclosure, and cryptographic attestations. Both camps claim alignment with public policy. Both reshape the monetary system. The question is not merely what rules apply, but where they reside—in organisational processes or in the protocol itself.

International coordination, the perennial headache of financial governance, complicates everything further. Payment flows are global; regulation is territorial. Countries export their rules through correspondent banking networks, sanctions regimes, and licensing requirements. Yet blockchains do not respect borders. A decentralised protocol can route value through dozens of jurisdictions without touching a supervised intermediary. Regulators fear this creates a shadow payment system immune to oversight. Developers counter that resilient, borderless networks protect citizens under repressive regimes. Both claims are true in different contexts, and therein lies the difficulty. The border post multiplies, and no single authority controls them all.

The uneven outcomes of this cross-border mismatch are already visible. Some jurisdictions pursue aggressive enforcement, treating any unlicensed activity as suspect by default. Others advertise regulatory "clarity" while quietly offering permissive environments. Arbitrage thrives. Firms structure themselves across multiple legal shelters: a compliance-heavy entity in London, a token-issuing arm in Zug, a liquidity hub in Singapore. The system disperses. At the same time, geopolitical tensions weaponise the financial system, using sanctions as tools of national strategy. This pushes some actors towards parallel networks, not out of ideology but necessity. Regulation becomes not only a domestic governance question but a geopolitical instrument.

Through all of this runs a deeper question: who controls the definition of money in a networked age? States assert authority through legal tender laws, supervisory powers, and enforcement tools. Protocol communities assert authority through code, consensus, and network effects. The regulatory wars are not battles over technicalities; they are contests over sovereignty. They determine whose rules define finality, whose signatures validate economic truth, and whose border posts the world must pass.

Yet it would be a mistake to read these conflicts as purely adversarial. Much of the coming regulatory architecture will emerge from hybridisation. Principle-based flexibility will blend with protocol-enforced controls. Perimeter lines will move from institutions to functions to flows. Compliance will become increasingly embedded, yet privacy-preserving techniques will prevent total auditability. Cross-border coordination will lag, but pockets of interoperability will emerge around common standards for custody, attestation, and risk. The result will not satisfy purists on either side. It will, however, shape how money moves for decades.

The chapter opens here, at the threshold of global contest. The regulatory wars are already reshaping not only the business models of crypto firms and financial institutions, but the fabric of financial citizenship itself. The question that hangs over the border post is simple, unsettling, and unavoidable: *when rules and networks collide, who yields, and who decides?*

Principle-Based versus Rule-Based

In March 2021, the UK Financial Conduct Authority convened an urgent call with several London-based crypto exchanges after a protocol upgrade on a major blockchain unexpectedly altered how transactions could be batched. The change broke nothing in the code; it broke a compliance interpretation. Under the FCA's long-standing *Client Assets Sourcebook*, operators must demonstrate that customer holdings remain segregated from firm funds. Yet the new batching method produced temporary pooling that the exchanges' lawyers feared could be construed as co-mingling. The FCA did not issue fresh guidance that week. Instead, it asked a question that revealed the deeper divide: "Explain how your controls uphold the principle of protecting client money, regardless of technical change." The exchanges wanted a checklist. The regulator wanted an argument. The moment captured the fault line that runs through the regulatory wars: whether fast-moving financial technologies can be governed by broad duties or must be pinned down through granular rules.

The paradox presents itself starkly. When a protocol can update within minutes yet a statutory instrument can take years, which approach—principles or rules—keeps pace? A five-word sentence applies here. Code outruns text. Each model of regulation responds differently to this tension. Principles promise adaptability but risk ambiguity. Rules promise clarity but risk obsolescence. Both try to steady a border post that technology continuously shifts.

A quiet motif threads through this terrain: the test. The test a regulator applies shapes the behaviour a firm adopts, the architecture a protocol builds, and the narrative a market internalises. And when the test fails to match the technology, the system buckles.

Principle-based regulation shows its strength in the FCA example. The regulator's insistence on upholding a duty—safeguard client assets—meant exchanges had room to propose new controls instead of waiting for rewritten checklists. This mirrors the approach of the UK Prudential Regulation Authority, which often relies on high-level obligations such as "maintain adequate financial resources" rather than prescribing thousands of pages of prescriptive metrics. It is flexible. It invites judgement. It moves with the market. The visible behaviour this produces is improvisation: firms convene emergency committees, adjust internal monitoring thresholds, and demonstrate that their intent aligns with supervisory expectations even as the technical terrain shifts under them.

But principles strain when novelty multiplies. A decentralised liquidity pool is not a broker, yet it matches orders. A hardware wallet never holds private keys, yet its firmware updates influence user risk. A staking service may allocate customer funds across multiple validators, raising questions about control and responsibility. Regulators ask whether these designs "act in the client's best interest", "manage conflicts", or "ensure operational resilience", but these phrases are thin guides when confronted with architecture that dissolves institutional boundaries entirely. Show a principle-based regime a DeFi protocol that has no directors, and it struggles to allocate responsibility. Name the challenge: decentralisation. Explain it: a system where no party fits the traditional accountabilities the law expects. The implication is sharp. A principle that cannot anchor accountability becomes an empty standard.

Rule-based frameworks attempt to correct for this. The European Securities and Markets Authority's approach to derivative reporting under EMIR, for instance, specifies exactly what data fields must be collected, how they must be formatted, and which entities must submit them. MiCA follows the same instinct: it prescribes capital requirements, licensing triggers, white paper disclosures, custody controls, and ongoing reporting obligations for crypto-asset service providers. The visible behaviour this produces is procedural discipline. Firms dedicate teams to mapping compliance fields to system outputs. Developers write code to adhere to specifications. Lawyers run flowcharts that determine licensing consequences.

Yet rules struggle when confronted with protocols that mutate silently. When Ethereum shifted from proof-of-work to proof-of-stake in September 2022, the economic characteristics of participation changed faster than any policy document could adapt. A validator's yield became a function of network conditions rather than mining economics. The EU's definitions of "virtual asset service provider" suddenly brushed against activities that might resemble collective investment undertakings. Here the rule-based approach falters. Name the limitation: rigidity. Explain it: rules drafted against static assumptions fail when the underlying technology rewrites those assumptions. The implication is structural. Rules drafted for yesterday's architecture constrain tomorrow's design.

A counter-example tempers this picture. The Monetary Authority of Singapore, often portrayed as rule-heavy, demonstrated agility in 2023 when it issued a detailed stablecoin framework that combined prescriptive reserve requirements with flexible governance expectations. It recognised that programmable, multi-issuer tokens demanded both clarity and adaptability. This hybrid model did not collapse under rapid protocol change; it adapted through engagement with technical details while leaving room for modular innovation. Reconciling this with earlier claims reveals the deeper truth: neither pure principles nor pure rules succeed alone when technology evolves too quickly. The border post moves, and the regulatory map must blend approaches to avoid incoherence.

The contrast becomes sharper when considering how each model copes with unpredictability. Principle-based regimes cope by demanding justification. When a protocol changes, a firm must show why its interpretation still aligns with the regulator's intent. This suits markets where institutions manage risks through judgement, and where supervisors trust firms to internalise broad obligations. Rule-based regimes cope by demanding alignment. When a protocol changes, a firm must show how its operations comply with listed requirements, often leading to technical patchwork. This suits markets where predictability and auditability dominate.

Rapid protocol change exposes both models. In 2020, when decentralised exchanges such as Uniswap and Sushiswap began processing billions in weekly volume, their automated market maker design undermined conventional distinctions between broker, dealer, and trading venue. Principle-based regimes asked whether the operators of front-end interfaces were "arranging deals". Rule-based regimes attempted to classify liquidity pools using existing categories designed for centralised intermediaries. Both approaches struggled, revealing an unmet need: a functional taxonomy that matches behaviour rather than institutional form.

Another example emerged during the FTX collapse in November 2022. Jurisdictions with principle-based regimes focused on failures of governance, segregation, and prudence. Jurisdictions with rule-based regimes emphasised breaches of specific licensing conditions. Both reached similar conclusions—catastrophic misconduct—but the mechanics differed. The practical implication matters: the model of regulation shapes not only oversight but the very narrative through which failure is understood. It shapes institutional trust and dictates reform trajectories.

The motif of the test returns. A principle is a narrative test: did the firm act responsibly? A rule is a mechanical test: did the firm follow the checklist? These tests direct market behaviour. In principle-led markets, firms optimise for defensibility. In rule-led markets, they optimise for documentation. Critically, neither guarantee outcomes. A firm may meet every rule yet still expose customers to unacceptable risk through untested code paths. A firm may honour every principle yet fall short of documentation that enables enforcement. The gap between compliance and safety widens in either model if the test does not align with technological reality.

Protocol change magnifies this gap. Consider a situation where a smart contract upgrade introduces new risk vectors. A rule-based regime might fail to detect the shift because the checklist does not include fields for that risk. A principle-based regime might rely on the firm's subjective assessment, which could vary widely. Neither approach inherently adapts to the technical nuance that a ten-line code change can shift billions in economic exposure. The implication is urgent: for digital assets, regulatory adaptability is not an abstract virtue but a functional necessity.

Yet adaptability must not come at the expense of certainty. Markets rely on predictable enforcement. Businesses rely on clear licensing triggers. Consumers rely on consistent protections. Here lies the unresolved tension. If principles dominate, firms must navigate grey zones that can chill innovation. If rules dominate, developers must freeze architectures to suit regulatory expectations, risking stagnation. The test, once again, becomes a border post. Too rigid, and the frontier closes. Too loose, and the frontier fractures.

The path ahead requires a recalibration of the relationship between these models. Principle-based frameworks need new interpretative scaffolding informed by technical expertise, not vague platitudes. Rule-based frameworks need modularity—a capacity to issue amendable technical schedules aligned with protocol evolution. Policymakers must recognise that neither moral exhortation nor procedural precision alone can govern programmable money.

The final question hangs unresolved: when the next protocol upgrade lands without warning, what should guide the regulatory response—flexible intent or fixed rule—and who decides which test applies?

Licences, Perimeters, and Grey Zones

On 25 June 2021, the UK Financial Conduct Authority issued a brief notice about a company that did not yet have a single retail customer: Binance Markets Limited, the British arm of the world's largest crypto exchange. From an office in Canary Wharf, the FCA stated that Binance was "not permitted to undertake any regulated activity in the UK". Overnight, high-street banks tightened card restrictions. Payment providers reviewed contracts. Social media filled with users asking why they could still trade on Binance.com if the regulator had "banned" Binance from the country. The answer sat in a subtle distinction. The FCA had drawn a line around *regulated activities.* Binance had stepped over that line in principle, but its core exchange sat legally elsewhere. The perimeter line looked thin.

That thinness matters. A licence is more than a rubber stamp; it is a decision that a certain activity falls inside a supervised zone. Outside that zone, other authorities may intervene—tax agencies, consumer protection bodies, criminal courts—but prudential and conduct oversight recede. Crypto forces regulators to redraw these lines under pressure. A self-custodial wallet used by a teenager in Manchester sits outside the perimeter. A centralised exchange that rehypothecates customer coins in Luxembourg sits inside. A DeFi interface hosted on a server in Amsterdam may float somewhere in between. The legal map is full of edges that do not quite join.

A quiet motif runs through this landscape: the threshold. Cross it and you accept scrutiny, capital rules, and audits. Stay below it and you may operate in a grey zone, tolerated until something goes wrong. The choice of where to place that threshold—especially around custody—structures the entire regulatory game.

In the UK and EU, perimeters have grown up around functions, not technologies. The UK's Regulated Activities Order, the EU's MiFID II, the Payment Services Directive, and now MiCA all define boxes: "safeguarding and administering investments", "operating a multilateral trading facility", "issuing electronic money", "providing virtual asset services". Supervisors then ask a simple but powerful question: *which box does this business fall into?* That question is not abstract. It decides whether a start-up in Berlin needs a full investment firm licence, a lighter crypto-asset service authorisation, or no licence at all.

Custody is where the threshold bites hardest. Show why with behaviour. When a UK-based fintech offers customers the ability to "buy Bitcoin" in-app, the legal analysis turns on who holds the keys. If the firm, or its appointed custodian, can move coins without the customer's consent, it likely falls within the "safeguarding and administering" perimeter. That triggers the Client Assets Sourcebook, capital requirements, and regular audits. If, by contrast, the app merely connects to a self-custodial wallet the user controls, regulators may treat it as unregulated software. The customer bears full risk. The difference between those two models is a line of remarkable consequence.

Why this intensity around custody? History. The collapse of Lehman Brothers in 2008 and the MF Global failure in 2011 seared a lesson into European supervisors: when client assets are commingled with firm capital or rehypothecated without restraint, losses cascade through the system. Client asset regimes were tightened. Segregation rules hardened. Reconciliation procedures were upgraded. Trust in markets rests heavily on the belief that, if an intermediary fails, customer property can be traced and returned.

Crypto custody challenges these assumptions. Assets sit on public ledgers, but control rests in private keys. A custodian can isolate those keys physically, slice them through multi-party computation, or scatter them across legal entities. It can also, as FTX demonstrated, quietly move them into proprietary trading accounts. Regulators therefore view any arrangement where a firm can sign on behalf of a customer as high-risk. Strict scrutiny follows: higher capital, sharper governance, detailed disclosure. The threshold is not ideological. It is empirical: who can move the money?

MiCA codifies this into a coherent perimeter. Under its terms, EU-based "crypto-asset service providers" that safekeep assets must obtain authorisation, meet capital thresholds, and implement robust organisational arrangements. The behaviour it encourages is visible: European exchanges restructure so that custody sits in segregated entities; large custodians seek multiple licences across member states; product teams rework flows to minimise the occasions on which the firm touches keys at all. The perimeter draws business models towards its own logic.

Yet grey zones remain. Consider a browser-based wallet whose code auto-updates from a server in Dublin. The project insists it is non-custodial; keys are generated client-side. But the update mechanism can, in theory, alter key derivation or subtly redirect transactions. Has the provider crossed the custody threshold? Does potential control matter as much as actual control? UK and EU law are used to dealing with trustees and nominees; they are less used to dealing with untrusted code pushed into user environments. Some supervisors respond by stretching conduct rules. Others remain cautious, waiting for test cases. The threshold blurs.

Perimeters also depend on how "investment" is defined. The German regulator BaFin, for example, chose early to treat certain tokens as financial instruments, bringing them under existing securities law. That decision pulled token custody into the same licensing regime as securities custody, with all its rigour. By contrast, before MiCA, many EU states treated utility tokens as outside financial regulation, focusing instead on anti-money-laundering rules. Custodians of such tokens fell into lighter-touch regimes, often under simple registration schemes. The same technical activity—holding a private key—thus attracted radically different levels of oversight depending on the token's legal label.

A credible counter-example sharpens this point. In the Netherlands, the central bank (DNB) initially required crypto service providers to verify ownership of every withdrawal address under strict AML interpretations. Wallet providers argued this went beyond EU law and pushed self-custodial users into friction-heavy channels. After legal challenge, DNB softened its stance, acknowledging that overly tight perimeters can drive activity into less visible forms. The limitation is instructive: a perimeter drawn too aggressively can erode the very oversight it seeks to strengthen.

Reconciliation lies in better mapping. Rather than asking merely "is this crypto?", regulators increasingly ask "what economic function does this activity perform?" Does it intermediate credit risk? Does it transform maturities? Does it pool and reallocate client assets? Does it provide systemic payment rails? Where answers are yes, perimeters tighten. Where no, lighter regimes apply. Under a generic UK/EU lens, this is evident in how stablecoin issuers are treated differently from pure software projects, and how custodial exchanges face more intrusive oversight than peer-to-peer marketplaces.

Activities around trading and advice present their own threshold issues. Is a Telegram channel run from Paris that shares "token research" providing investment advice? If it charges subscription fees and moves markets, an EU supervisor might say yes. Does a Discord server that coordinates liquidity mining across multiple protocols operate an unlicensed collective investment scheme? The legal instincts say perhaps; the practical enforcement capacity says not yet. These fringes of activity exist in jurisdictional penumbra. Supervisors pick battles selectively, focusing on large, systemically relevant actors. Smaller players inhabit the grey, learning where the line lies by watching who gets prosecuted.

There is another, quieter reason custody attracts special attention: political optics. When a central bank governor or finance minister is asked whether citizens' digital assets are safe, the question invariably concerns custodial failures, not bad trades. Regulators can plausibly respond that they do not police market risk in speculative assets. They cannot plausibly accept a pattern of custodial collapses that wipe out retail savings. The threshold between self-directed risk and custodial failure is thus politically charged. It determines where blame falls when headlines turn hostile.

Perimeters also express values about autonomy. The UK's approach to self-custody has so far been relatively hands-off: owning a hardware wallet or running a node is not a regulated activity. The EU's texts, including MiCA and AML directives, similarly focus on intermediaries, not individuals. This choice is normative. It treats the citizen as capable of holding value directly, outside licensed channels. But as programmable money becomes more pervasive, that stance may be tested. If self-custody at scale undermines AML goals or complicates sanctions enforcement, some policymakers may argue for pulling more of the ecosystem inside formal perimeters. The threshold would move closer to the individual.

The motif of the threshold returns here with more urgency. Perimeters must balance three pressures: protect consumers; preserve financial stability; avoid smothering innovation. Place the line too close to the core, and unregulated shadows expand. Place it too wide, and every developer must become a quasi-bank. The UK/EU approach—licensing custody and key intermediation tightly while leaving pure software and self-custody outside—tries to strike that balance. It is imperfect. It will be contested.

Operationally, these boundaries shape architecture. A French start-up designing a new wallet must decide whether to hold any recovery data server-side. A single design decision can tip it from unregulated tool to regulated custodian. A Spanish exchange weighing whether to offer staking-as-a-service must decide whether to pool customers' assets or simply facilitate delegation. One path demands a full MiCA licence and possibly AIFMD analysis. The other might sit under a lighter regime. Legal advice becomes product design. The perimeter draws the blueprint.

Yet technology has its own logic. Developers find ways to modularise custody; to separate user interfaces from key management; to design contracts where neither they nor any single party can move funds unilaterally. These patterns aim to keep activity below regulatory thresholds while still delivering convenience. Some are clever workarounds; others are genuine innovations that reduce custodial risk. Regulators watch warily, deciding which to bless and which to challenge. Each decision redraws the line.

The unresolved tension is straightforward but difficult. As digital asset markets grow, more economic activity will sit close to these thresholds. The question for policymakers is not simply where to place them once, but how to move them as architecture evolves without jolting markets or driving users into the dark. And for builders, a different question persists: when a single line on a regulatory map can transform your product into a financial institution overnight, how much power should that line have—and who, precisely, should hold the pen?

Compliance as Architecture

On 21 June 2019, in a conference room overlooking Lake Geneva, the Financial Action Task Force (FATF) adopted a short paragraph that sent developers scrambling across the world. In its updated Recommendation 16, the body urged countries to ensure that "virtual asset service providers" transmitted originator and beneficiary information alongside transfers above a set threshold. It was an old idea in a new setting: the travel rule, born for correspondent banking, now aimed at crypto. Within months, exchanges in London, Frankfurt, and Paris found that their technical roadmaps had acquired a new, non-negotiable feature. Compliance could no longer be confined to policy binders and training sessions. It had to live in code.

The paradox was immediately clear to anyone who had ever copied a Bitcoin address. Blockchains broadcast value movements, not names. Traditional banks used SWIFT messages to carry structured identity data; virtual asset transfers, by design, carried none. To comply with the travel rule, firms would have to bolt a second messaging layer onto the first, or redesign their core flows so that compliant transactions became the default. The question ceased to be "what fields does the regulation require?" and became "what must the system *remember* about each user, each transfer, each counterparty?" Architecture turned into law's first line of enforcement.

A quiet motif runs through this subchapter: the tag. Every design choice decides what tags follow a transaction—who sent it, through whom, with which credentials—and who can read them. In analogue systems, tags lived on paper forms and internal ledgers. In digital systems, tags live in databases and standards. In programmable systems, they risk being fused to the money itself.

Compliance has always left architectural fingerprints. The paper world used stamped forms, internal account numbers, and physical customer files. The early electronic world used message formats. SWIFT's MT103 payment message, which became standard in the 1990s, includes specific fields for ordering customer, beneficiary, and intermediaries. These were not mere technical conveniences; they encoded regulatory expectations about traceability. Payment systems were built so that the necessary data could travel. Banks did not tack on compliance after the fact. They embedded it into the way wires were sent.

FATF's 2019 decision forced crypto intermediaries to do something similar. Industry bodies responded by drafting a common data language, the InterVASP Messaging Standard IVMS101, agreed in 2020 by a consortium of firms in London, Zurich, and Singapore. IVMS101 defined how to represent originator and beneficiary information—names, addresses, account identifiers—in a JSON-like structure that could be sent between virtual asset service providers (VASPs). Show, name, explain, implication: the standard showed that travel-rule data could be structured; it was named as a neutral, open specification; it explained a path for VASPs to talk to each other about customers without touching the blockchain; and it implied a new reality—crypto compliance would increasingly live in messaging protocols, SDKs, and APIs, not only in manuals.

The architectural turn goes deeper than data formats. Once regulators define obligations—screen customers, monitor transactions, trace flows—product designers decide *where* to satisfy them. A UK-based exchange might implement strict know-your-customer checks at onboarding and allow unrestricted withdrawals to any address. A European custodian might choose a different pattern: light onboarding but heavy screening of withdrawal addresses, using chain-analytics tools to score risk. Both satisfy formal AML rules. Yet they produce different systems. In one, friction appears at the door. In the other, friction appears at the exit. The tag moves.

The implications are concrete. Users learn that interacting with certain platforms requires deep disclosure; interacting with others requires less. High-risk customers gravitate to the latter. Low-risk customers tolerate more friction. Over time, architectural choices sort populations. Compliance becomes a sorting machine.

Custody is where architecture and obligation intertwine most tightly. A custodian that holds private keys can block transfers, insert additional checks, or implement time-locks that allow further review. The same is not true for a self-hosted wallet. For this reason, UK and EU policymakers have focused much of their AML energy on intermediaries that can *interfere* with the flow of funds. The travel rule itself, as transposed into European law, applies primarily to transfers between obliged entities: between two exchanges, or between an exchange and a custodian. The behavioural consequence is visible: European firms build internal address books, whitelisting counterparties that have implemented compatible travel-rule messaging. Transfers to "unhosted" wallets are either heavily monitored or capped, even where not legally required, because firms fear supervisory criticism. The architecture favours known tags.

Yet there is a credible counter-example. Some jurisdictions, particularly smaller EU member states in the early implementation phase of AMLD5, focused more on registration and basic KYC than on fully fledged travel-rule execution. Local exchanges could operate with simpler setups: basic manual record-keeping, limited interoperability, shallow integration with global standards. Their systems did not embed the same level of metadata. This created pockets of lighter architecture within a broader, tightening regime. Arbitrage followed. Users who disliked intrusive data collection routed flows through these pockets. The limitation is obvious: compliance that lives only in local architecture cannot easily police global behaviour.

Privacy-preserving compliance efforts are an attempt to escape this trade-off. If architecture must carry tags, can it carry them in a way that limits who can read them, and when? Researchers in Europe and the UK have explored variants of "zero-knowledge KYC": systems in which a user proves, cryptographically, that they have been verified by an approved provider without revealing underlying identity attributes. In such models, a wallet address might be associated with a reusable proof that its owner passed KYC with a regulated entity in, say, Frankfurt, without disclosing the owner's name on-chain. The tag exists. It is just not legible to everyone.

Show this approach, name its actors, explain the mechanics, draw implications. Privacy-preserving projects—whether academic consortia, industry coalitions, or pilot CBDC designs—tend to build around three behaviours. First, they create credential issuers: banks, e-money institutions, or dedicated KYC providers that vouch for users. Secondly, they build wallets or smart contracts that can verify proofs without learning the underlying data. Thirdly, they define governance rules for when authorities may pierce anonymity—for example, with a court order. The implication is ambitious: a system where most transactions remain unlinkable to identities, but sufficiently grave concerns can trigger targeted de-anonymisation through due process.

This is not science fiction. The European Central Bank's early experiments with a digital euro explicitly mentioned "anonymity vouchers" in some prototypes: tokens that allowed small payments without identity checks, while larger transactions would require stronger verification. The Swiss National Bank's Helvetia project explored wholesale CBDC structures where participants could prove membership of regulated categories without replaying full KYC every time. In both cases, compliance logic was baked into design choices about how wallets, nodes, and messaging layers functioned. Architecture did the work.

Still, there are hard limits. Zero-knowledge proofs, secure enclaves, and selective disclosure mechanisms come with computational and operational costs. They demand more complex key management, more careful software engineering, and more sophisticated incident response. For a resource-constrained start-up in Tallinn or Lisbon, the temptation is strong to implement the simplest possible architecture: full data collection, centralised storage, straightforward API calls to analytics vendors. That path meets regulatory checklists and minimises engineering complexity, but it also maximises the attack surface and entrenches data hoarding. The tag becomes heavy and promiscuous, available to anyone who breaches a database or obtains a warrant.

A second tension lies in the incentives of public authorities. Law enforcement agencies often seek broader access to data, not narrower. They favour architectures that generate and retain rich metadata. Anonymity vouchers sound acceptable on paper; in practice, there is pressure to lower thresholds or expand log retention when threats emerge. The architecture that once balanced privacy and oversight slowly shifts towards total visibility. The tag grows.

We have seen this movie before. The expansion of "know your customer" regimes in the 1990s and 2000s gradually normalised extensive identity checks for routine financial activity. What began as a tool against serious crime became a baseline expectation for opening a current account or mobile wallet. The architectural counterpart was the proliferation of centralised KYC databases and blacklists. In the crypto context, a similar drift is plausible: architectures built with careful privacy controls could be relaxed under political and security pressures. What starts as "selective disclosure in exceptional cases" can become "routine access for authorised agencies".

There is, however, a powerful countervailing force: data protection law. The EU's General Data Protection Regulation (GDPR) imposes principles of data minimisation and purpose limitation. Firms must collect only what is necessary and retain it only as long as needed. Supervisory authorities have already scrutinised some AML practices through that lens. If architects design systems that hoard far more metadata than required, they may find themselves criticised by privacy regulators even as financial regulators urge vigilance. Compliance as architecture becomes a tug-of-war between two legal regimes.

This interplay affects protocol design in subtle ways. Consider a stablecoin issuer headquartered in Paris. If it chooses to embed address-blacklisting directly into its smart contract, allowing it to freeze individual addresses at will, it creates an extremely powerful compliance lever. At the same time, it raises difficult questions: what criteria trigger a freeze? How is that decision documented? Does the issuer become a quasi-enforcement arm for any authority that sends it a request? Architects must decide whether to implement the simplest control—hard freezes—or more nuanced measures, such as time-locked restrictions or multi-party approval schemes that require, say, both issuer and court to sign. Each design reflects a view about how obligations should operate.

DeFi protocols confront similar choices when integrating with the regulated world. A lending pool that wishes to accept deposits from a licensed European exchange might implement allow-lists at the smart contract level, admitting only addresses that present compliant credentials. The alternative is to remain permissionless, letting any address interact, and leave compliance to the access points—the exchanges and wallets. The first option builds compliance into the protocol; the second keeps it at the edge. In architectural terms, the tag either travels with the asset or stays at the gateway.

Neither approach is fully comfortable. Protocol-level controls risk ossifying rules that may change; upgrading contracts to reflect new regulations is non-trivial. Edge-level controls, by contrast, may prove porous: once an asset leaves a compliant venue and enters the wider network, its further path becomes harder to constrain. Yet the choice cannot be avoided. Every live system today embodies one or the other philosophy, even if its builders never put it in those terms.

The motif of the tag returns with force here. A payment is no longer just an amount, an asset, and a destination. It is also a bundle of attributes: who has seen this user's passport, which risk scores have been computed, which sanctions lists were checked, which logs were kept, and for how long. Architectures that treat tags as separate from the asset—kept in side-channels, handled by regulated entities—preserve some of the neutrality of base protocols. Architectures that weld tags into the asset—by design or by practice—turn money into a carrier of identity by default.

The unresolved tension sits precisely there. As programmable money spreads, societies must decide where they want compliance to live: in law and institutional practice, or in code and protocol design. If they choose the latter too eagerly, they risk making every unit of value a surveillance device. If they cling to the former without adaptation, they risk leaving regulators blind to genuinely dangerous flows. The question for architects, regulators, and citizens alike is disarmingly simple: when you send money, how much of *you* should travel with it, and who gets to decide?

International Coordination, Uneven Outcomes

In April 2021, the Monetary Authority of Singapore (MAS) issued a notice that caught international exchanges off-guard. By tightening exemptions under the Payment Services Act, MAS required firms serving local users to meet stricter AML and technology-risk standards within months. The result was swift and measurable: several exchanges based in Hong Kong and Seoul blocked new registrations from Singaporean residents, citing compliance burdens and licensing delays. Some withdrew entirely. Others shifted servers to jurisdictions with more forgiving supervisory regimes. A line of code written in Singapore changed business decisions in London and liquidity patterns in Zurich. Money moved fast; rules did not.

Why did a single regulatory move in one city-state unsettle firms across three continents? Because digital assets ignore borders as a matter of design, while regulatory mandates cling to geography. A paradox emerges: the faster the transfer, the more sluggish the consensus. The global financial system has always wrestled with the mismatch between cross-border flows and national oversight, but crypto sharpens the mismatch to a point. A user in Warsaw can route value to a counterparty in Buenos Aires within minutes. A supervisory college may take months to agree on a shared definition of "custody". Borders hold regulators in place even as protocols stitch markets together.

A quiet motif threads through this subchapter: the line. Jurisdictional lines, definitional lines, supervisory lines—each drawn differently, each forcing market participants to choose where to sit. Some lines protect. Others distort. All travel badly.

The global architecture of financial regulation has long relied on coordination bodies such as the Financial Stability Board (FSB) and the FATF. Their recommendations travel through diplomatic channels, consultation processes, and domestic legislation. In traditional finance, the system more or less copes because instruments and intermediaries map cleanly onto established categories. A bond is a bond. A bank is a bank. But a decentralised liquidity pool or a distributed validator set does not respect neat compartments. When FATF updated its guidance in June 2019 to cover "virtual asset service providers", it left national authorities to decide how to interpret edge cases: protocol developers, non-custodial wallets, miners, validators. The guidance moved in one stroke. Its implementation moved in dozens.

Show, name, explain, implication. Europe took the path of legislative precision, culminating in the Markets in Crypto-Assets Regulation (MiCA) adopted in 2023. It defined "crypto-asset service providers" with specific categories—custody, exchange operations, advice—and tied each to licensing and capital requirements. The United Kingdom, by contrast, opted for a staged expansion of the regulated perimeter, beginning with AMLD5 transposition in 2020, later supplemented by the Financial Services and Markets Act 2023, and relying heavily on FCA guidance to interpret duties for firms that straddle old and new models. The implication was immediate: firms comfortable with structured, passportable EU rules tended to gravitate towards continental hubs; firms seeking supervisory dialogue and flexibility often stayed within the UK's evolving framework. The line split markets.

The United States provided a further contrast. Between 2021 and 2023, enforcement actions by the Securities and Exchange Commission (SEC) and the Commodity Futures Trading Commission (CFTC) turned definitional debates into de facto policy. Was a token an investment contract? Did staking services constitute unregistered securities offerings? Instead of adopting a bespoke regime, US authorities interpreted crypto through existing statutes, leaving classification uncertain and dynamic. The limitation is stark: such enforcement-led approaches create uneven signals and force firms to invest heavily in legal interpretation. Some accepted the cost. Others, particularly European-origin firms, chose to exit the US or wall off American users altogether. Regulatory arbitrage became a structural feature, not a fringe strategy.

There is, however, a credible counter-example that tempers the narrative of unbridled divergence. Switzerland, through the Federal Council and FINMA, adopted a coherent digital-asset framework early, codifying token categories and the duties tied to custody and trading. By 2021, major institutions in Zurich could rely on a stable, predictable perimeter. The country became a hub for both decentralised protocol foundations and regulated custodians. It shows that national clarity can attract activity even when global harmonisation lags. But this does not resolve the underlying problem: Switzerland can be precise about its own rules; it cannot guarantee that its rules align with those of France, Singapore, or Brazil. The line stays local.

Coordination challenges reveal themselves most clearly in cross-border investigations. A European exchange may freeze assets flagged as suspicious via chain analytics, only to discover that a partner jurisdiction lacks comparable definitions or thresholds for red flags. Metrics that trigger a review in Amsterdam—a sanctioned address, a mixer link, a darknet correlation—may not trigger anything in Dubai. Firms measure risk according to local mandates but interact with global flows. The mismatch produces gaps. It also creates incentives for routing transactions through friendlier corridors. The infamous "regulatory shopping" that shaped payments and gambling in the 2000s reappears here, now applied to digital-asset custody and token issuance.

Design choices amplify or dampen these mismatches. Consider stablecoin issuers operating across multiple jurisdictions. An issuer headquartered in Paris may implement strict blacklisting procedures to satisfy MiCA, blocking dozens of addresses per quarter. A sister entity in a Caribbean jurisdiction may apply a lighter rubric, intervening only when compelled by direct requests. Users learn the pattern. They choose which issuer's tokens to hold and which to avoid. The behaviour is rational: a token's compliance profile becomes part of its value. The motif of the line appears again. One token carries heavy constraints; another floats more freely. But both circulate in the same pools, the same DeFi protocols, the same wallets. A global asset with local obligations cannot help but produce uneven outcomes.

Cross-border consensus lags for structural reasons that are not easily solved. Domestic politics shape regulatory priorities. The European Union emphasises consumer protection, prudential oversight, and market integrity. Singapore emphasises operational resilience and AML controls. The United States emphasises investor protection through the lens of securities law. These priorities express different histories and institutional philosophies. They yield different policy instruments. Even if regulators agree on the end—safer markets—they disagree on the path: principle-based supervision, detailed licensing, prescriptive technical standards, or enforcement-led deterrence. The lines reflect identities as much as mandates.

There is also a deeper technical constraint. Protocols evolve faster than treaties or directives. A cross-border consensus process, such as a FATF plenary or FSB working group, might meet semi-annually. A major protocol upgrade—Ethereum's Merge in September 2022, for example—can rewrite the underlying economic mechanics in a single event. When consensus mechanisms shift, when new privacy layers emerge, when new bridges proliferate, regulatory bodies struggle to update positions with comparable speed. The result is predictable: the protocol moves; the perimeter stays; arbitrage thrives.

But uneven outcomes are not merely a function of regulatory lag. They emerge because private actors actively exploit mismatches. Exchanges reroute order flow through subsidiaries in more permissive jurisdictions. Custodians incorporate in countries with light-touch oversight to minimise capital requirements. Token issuers shop for auditors and legal opinions that fit desired classifications. Decentralised autonomous organisations (DAOs) incorporate as foundations in Zug or the Cayman Islands to shield core developers from liability risks elsewhere. These choices are not accidents. They are strategies informed by lines on maps.

The counter-example that complicates this narrative lies in collaborative supervisory colleges. The European Banking Authority (EBA) and the European Securities and Markets Authority (ESMA) have experimented with cross-border monitoring teams for crypto firms with multi-country operations. These colleges share data, coordinate inspections, and attempt to apply consistent standards. Early reports from 2022 to 2023 show that such coordination can reduce arbitrage by aligning supervisory expectations even without full harmonisation. But coordination of this kind remains rare and resource-intensive. It does not scale easily to the hundreds of exchanges, custodians, and issuers that populate the market. The gap between ambition and implementation remains large.

The place where mismatches become most acute is sanctions. When the US Treasury's Office of Foreign Assets Control (OFAC) sanctioned Tornado Cash addresses in August 2022, custodians in Frankfurt implemented near-instant blocks. Exchanges in Tokyo followed. But in several jurisdictions, authorities questioned whether a smart contract could be sanctioned at all under domestic law. The result was a fragmented response: some firms blocked deposits automatically; others accepted them but monitored outflows; others ignored the sanctions entirely. A single enforcement action fractured global patterns of liquidity and forced protocols to confront an uncomfortable reality: compliance with one jurisdiction's rules can create exposure in another. The line becomes a fracture.

A pattern emerges across these examples. The more global the asset, the more local the obligations; the more local the obligations, the more global the arbitrage. The system oscillates. Actors seek predictability, but predictability is scarce when every border introduces a new interpretation of custody, a new definition of a virtual asset service provider, a new list of prohibited addresses.

The motif of the line returns in a final, sharper form. Every attempt to coordinate—guidance documents, cross-border working groups, mutual recognition arrangements—tries to straighten lines drawn at different angles. Yet money moves diagonally. It routes around obstacles. It finds weak points. It tests every seam.

The unresolved tension is straightforward but profound. Should the world aim for a uniform global regime for digital-asset oversight, accepting the political cost of ceding discretion? Or should it embrace regulatory diversity, accepting arbitrage as the price of national autonomy? Neither path is comfortable, and both demand trade-offs. The reader is left with a question that regulators can no longer avoid: when digital value crosses twenty borders in a minute, who draws the line that matters, and how long will it hold?

Chapter 7
Global South, Global Stakes

The mother stands in the shade of a corrugated zinc awning, her phone held tight in her palm as the midday heat presses down on Kumasi. She has waited forty-three minutes for the text confirming that the money sent from her brother in Milan has finally cleared. The payment itself was modest—€120—and the fee meant she received less than she expected. Worse, the cedi slid again overnight. Before she has even withdrawn the cash, its purchasing power has already thinned. When the message arrives at last, she exhales, pockets the phone, and walks briskly to the market where tomatoes have risen in price since last week. The transfer was meant to stabilise her household. It landed into volatility instead.

Stories like hers rarely appear in policy papers or conference keynotes, yet they reveal the stakes of financial architecture more clearly than any institutional chart. In Accra, Manila, Tegucigalpa, Karachi, and beyond, families navigate a choreography of fees, queues, delays, and devaluations that wealthier nations forgot long ago. For hundreds of millions, money is not merely a medium of exchange; it is an unpredictable companion—supportive some months, treacherous in others. Where remittances are lifelines rather than luxuries, the reliability of rails is a matter of dignity.

Here lies the chapter's proposition: much of the world meets money not through banks or brokers but through movement—flows across borders, between relatives, across informal markets, between cash and mobile balances, between trust and experiment. This movement is the centre of gravity for the Global South, and it is here that the contest between Bitcoin and banks becomes most visceral. Not theoretical. Not speculative. Immediate.

To speak of the Global South is not to flatten its diversity. Inflation in Argentina is not the same creature as inflation in

Nigeria. The labour migrations connecting the Philippines and the Gulf states differ from those linking Venezuela and Colombia. The informal economies of Kenya, Bangladesh, and Peru share family traits but not destinies. Yet across these differences runs a common thread: when formal institutions falter, people improvise; when currencies wobble, families adapt; when financial networks exclude, communities build their own rails.

This tension—between institutional fragility and grassroots resilience—animates the chapter. Remittances anchor the opening because they expose every fracture in the present system. High fees imposed by entrenched intermediaries. Disbursement delays that undercut urgency. Currency risks borne entirely by the recipient. These frictions sketch the lived landscape against which any alternative technology must be judged. Digital assets enter that story not as ideological symbols but as practical experiments in reducing drag: faster settlement, lower fees, fewer gatekeepers. Yet for every promise, there is a risk, and the household in Kumasi does not have the margin for speculative missteps.

From remittances we turn to informality—a domain often dismissed by technocrats yet indispensable to billions. In many countries, the majority of adults cannot meet the identity or documentation requirements demanded by banks. Thin credit files, inconsistent addresses, unregistered employment, and patchy records leave them outside the perimeter of traditional finance. In such contexts, trust is brokered through people rather than paperwork. A mobile number stands in for a passport; a community group substitutes for a credit bureau; a shared handset becomes a family treasury. Bitcoin, with its reliance on keys rather than credentials, sits oddly yet intriguingly alongside these realities. It promises inclusion by design but demands digital competence that informal networks must build collectively, often in environments where misinformation circulates faster than guidance.

The chapter moves next to resource states, where money and minerals intertwine in ways that unsettle conventional economic logic. In oil-rich countries from Angola to Azerbaijan, fiscal cycles rise and fall with global commodity prices. When revenues surge, governments spend; when prices collapse, currencies weaken and external debt balloons. These oscillations colour public attitudes towards both domestic banking systems and foreign-denominated assets. Bitcoin enters this terrain as both an escape valve and a provocation. Its fixed supply appeals to citizens fatigued by inflationary cycles. Its volatility repels policymakers tasked with stabilising budgets or defending exchange rates. And for states accustomed to rentier models—where control over resource flows sustains political authority—the idea of a decentralised, non-sovereign asset is doubly disruptive. It threatens not only monetary orthodoxy but also entrenched political bargains.

Finally, we confront the knife-edge choice facing many emerging economies: to leapfrog or to lock in. Mobile-first payment systems across East Africa and South Asia show what leapfrogging can achieve. Entire populations bypassed legacy banking infrastructure and embraced digital wallets, QR codes, and peer-to-peer transfers with remarkable speed. This created new forms of financial participation and catalysed micro-enterprises that banks would never have financed. Yet leapfrogging comes with its own dependencies. A handful of telecom operators become de facto financial gatekeepers. National payment switches centralise risk. Commercial incentives collide with public goods. And once established, dominant platforms can harden into structures as rigid as the ones they replaced. The question is no longer whether technology can open doors—it can—but whether it will open enough of them, in the right places, for the right people.

Threaded throughout is a recurring motif: the balance between fragility and agency. The Global South is often described through the former, as a patchwork of vulnerabilities. Yet this chapter emphasises the latter—the ingenuity with which communities navigate scarcity, the ease with which they adopt tools that solve real problems, the creativity with which they blend old practices and new technologies. This agency shapes adoption curves more decisively than white papers or academic models. It turns protocols into livelihoods or liabilities. It defines whether Bitcoin becomes a complement, a competitor, or a footnote.

We will move through remittance corridors, informal settlements, resource capitals, and mobile-money economies not to romanticise them but to understand the stakes. For much of the world, the future of money is not an intellectual puzzle but a daily negotiation. The financial system of the next decade will affect where families eat, where young people migrate, where governments invest, and where political power consolidates or fractures. The Global South, often treated as the periphery of monetary debates, is in fact their centre of gravity.

The question waiting at the chapter's end—one that policymakers and protocol designers alike continue to wrestle with—is deceptively simple: when financial tools evolve faster than institutions, who gains the most from the change, and who risks being left with the bill?

Remittances and Everyday Volatility: When local currency wobbles, options matter. A family remittance vignette shows fees, delays, and devaluation shaping risk.

The exchange queue outside Banco de la Nación in Buenos Aires stretched halfway around the block on 12 January 2023. A young nurse, Mariela, stood near the front, gripping the receipt for the US$200 her brother had sent from Barcelona the night before. By the time she reached the counter, the peso had slipped again. The teller revised the rate. She received roughly ten per cent less than she expected. She did not

protest. She simply folded the notes into a worn purse, walked to a nearby kiosk, and paid the gas bill before the price adjustment scheduled for later in the week. Her brother had sent money to stabilise her month. The system had shaved value at every stage: a €7 fee at the sending agent, a twenty-hour settlement delay, and a fresh round of devaluation on arrival. She left with less certainty than she brought into the queue.
Five words form the quiet motif of this subchapter: *speed alters economic outcomes.* In remittance corridors, even hours matter. When currencies wobble at the pace of Argentina's, Ghana's, or Lebanon's in specific periods, families learn to measure time in exchange-rate losses. The delay is not abstract. It appears in real behaviours: the rush to withdraw before new controls, the hunt for dollar shops, the bargaining at produce markets as prices rise twice in a week. Remittances are framed as financial flows in policy papers; lived experience reveals them as temporal contests. Whoever controls the clock gains the surplus.

Mariela's case illustrates more than hardship. It exemplifies the structure of risk transferred silently onto families. To show this, we begin with a simple observation: remittance systems treat money as if it were stable while the people who depend on it inhabit environments where stability is a daily reference point, not a default condition. The World Bank measured global average remittance fees at 6.2 per cent in 2022 (World Bank Remittance Prices Worldwide, 2022). That is a metric. But the human metric is different: families lose entire days' wages to intermediary tolls before a single note reaches home. When the receiving currency is sliding, fees become levies on survival.

This brings us to the first major claim. Show: queues at remittance counters fill long before dawn in Harare, Lagos, and Dhaka. Name: Ecocash in Zimbabwe, for example, saw surging inbound digital transfers during the 2019 currency crisis as residents sought any mechanism to bypass cash shortages. Explain: digital rails reduce the physical friction but do not remove price risk. If the inflow takes twenty-four hours to land, the gap between the sender's intention and the recipient's reality widens. Implication: design choices that appear trivial in stable-currency economies—batch settlement, weekend closures, redundant compliance checks—carry amplified consequences where economic time is compressed.

A second case sharpens this contrast. In Manila in 2020, Overseas Filipino Workers (OFWs) sending money from Riyadh often faced multi-hop transfers routed through correspondent banks in New York before returning to Asia. The structure was not malicious; it was path dependence in the plumbing of global finance. But each hop imposed fees and extended delays. When COVID-19 lockdowns tightened, incomes fell across the Gulf. Families in the Philippines suddenly faced the double risk of shrinking remittances *and* deteriorating conversion rates. The visible behaviour here was stark: more households cashed out immediately rather than leaving funds in mobile wallets, fearing sudden peso slippage. This underscores the chapter's recurring image: people racing the clock.

Now we introduce a counter-example, credible and real, to avoid romanticising alternatives. El Salvador's 2021 Bitcoin law, enacted in San Salvador in September, promised zero-fee digital remittances and near-instant settlement via state-backed wallets. Tens of thousands experimented with the system in its first months. Some received transfers more quickly than ever before. Yet volatility cut both ways. A family expecting US$150 worth of bitcoin saw its value swing by US$20 in a week. For recipients living close to subsistence, this instability rivalled the very currency risk they hoped to escape. The limitation is clear: faster rails remove friction, but they do not neutralise volatility in the asset being used as the rail. Reconciling this with the Philippine and Argentinian cases yields a deeper insight: the optimal remittance tool must minimise both extraction *and* oscillation. That is a harder target than it appears.

Having anchored the examples, we shift to structural reasoning. Remittance risk stems from three interacting decisions. First, the sender chooses a corridor—retail agent, mobile app, or crypto transfer. Second, intermediaries determine routing—through correspondent banks, settlement hubs, or decentralised networks. Third, the recipient decides when to convert, withdraw, or hold. Each decision maps directly onto a visible behaviour: choosing Saturday morning to avoid Monday price resets; converting half immediately and holding half in a stablecoin; splitting a transfer between cash and mobile balance. These behaviours reveal not just personal preference but embedded distrust in the rhythm of local currencies.

Trust appears here not as sentiment but as a metric: the spread between official and street exchange rates. In Lebanon during its 2020–2021 crisis, that spread exceeded 500 per cent at one point. When spreads widen, trust collapses. When trust collapses, families arbitrage between rails—formal, informal, mobile, crypto, dollar cash. The decision is never ideological. It is practical. They commit to whatever option reduces loss velocity.

A second structural layer concerns remittance providers themselves. Western Union, MoneyGram, and newer entrants like Remitly adopt compliance frameworks shaped by regulators in Washington, Brussels, and London. To show this, consider that Western Union temporarily paused services in certain high-risk corridors after sanctions updates in February 2022. Name: Western Union's decision affected transfers to Russia and Belarus. Explain: providers must update sanction filters, anti-money-laundering checks, and correspondent relationships whenever rulebooks shift. Implication: political decisions far from the remittance corridor alter life for families with no influence over them.

This political overhang is a form of systemic friction masked as prudence.

A third claim concerns the rise of dollarised stablecoins in Latin America and parts of Africa. USDC and USDT transfers into Lagos, Mexico City, and Buenos Aires surged between mid-2020 and late 2022, according to public blockchain analytics from Chainalysis (2022). Show: people increasingly receive remittances directly into crypto wallets. Name: in Nigeria, stablecoin inflows into retail wallets grew markedly after the Central Bank's 2021 restrictions on cryptocurrency exchanges. Explain: users sought workarounds to both banking limits and naira volatility. Implication: the informal adoption of digital dollars signals a new hierarchy of trust—one that relies on private issuers rather than domestic banks. The risks are clear: issuer failure, depegging, and regulatory intervention could unwind benefits rapidly. Yet recipients treat these risks as probabilistic; immediate stability often outweighs theoretical tail risks when the local currency weakens daily.

The chapter's motif—*speed alters economic outcomes*—reappears when we consider settlement timing. A remittance arriving on a Monday during capital controls behaves differently from one landing on a Friday afternoon. When Turkish inflation surged past 60 per cent in mid-2022 (TurkStat, 2022), households began tracking not just rates but hours of the day when bureaucratic restrictions tightened. Some kept cash under mattresses; others leaned on informal hawala networks that settled instantly. Hawala illustrates the counter-example's reconciliation: informal systems may outperform both banks and blockchains in speed, yet they depend heavily on social reputation rather than legal recourse. Their strength becomes fragility in a dispute.

We must also examine the psychological dimension—without drifting into generalisation. Recipients often display ultra-short-term decision-making not because they lack planning skills but because they inhabit monetary environments that punish patience. A mother in Caracas who converts dollars to bolívares only when necessary demonstrates rational hedging, not impulsivity. In such settings, bitcoin adoption appears in micro-decisions: holding a small portion of a remittance overnight to preserve value, despite volatility; experimenting with Lightning transfers because they bypass intermediaries; using bitcoin to pay a landlord who prefers a hard asset to the collapsing local currency. Yet these cases remain pockets, not yet mainstream, because the volatility of bitcoin competes with the volatility of the local currency. Stability beats ideology every time.

We should also name the geopolitical layer. The U.S. dollar's dominance in remittance corridors shapes both options and constraints. El Salvador's 2001 decision to dollarise locked its economy into the monetary policies of a nation it does not influence. That stability attracted remittance corridors from Los Angeles and Houston, but it also meant that any digital alternative would be judged against the dollar, not its volatile predecessor. Likewise, in Argentina, the informal "dólar blue" market exemplifies the spread between what money *ought* to be and what it *is* at the counter. These cases force a sharper question: if bitcoin or stablecoins step into remittance roles, do they complement or challenge the dollar's gravitational pull?

As we approach the chapter's end, the structural motif connects back to lived experience. Every option—bank, mobile wallet, hawala, stablecoin, bitcoin—carries a different configuration of fees, speed, volatility, and risk. Each maps onto behaviours that define economic life: rushing to the market before prices shift; splitting transfers across currencies; keeping multiple apps to arbitrage rails. The families who navigate these choices are not passive recipients of global monetary flows. They are portfolio managers of necessity, balancing uncertainty with ingenuity.

The unresolved tension is simple yet sharp: if speed truly alters outcomes, and if volatility punishes delay, which remittance rail—old or new—minimises loss while maximising dignity? The answer will define not only household stability but also the emerging monetary order in the places where stakes are highest.

Informality, Inclusion, and Trust: Banks avoid thin files; networks accept keys. We compare onboarding frictions and community education.

In March 2016, at a small branch of Absa Bank in Soweto, a street vendor named Thandi waited nearly an hour to open a basic account. She presented her South African ID, proof of address, and her trading permit. The clerk examined each document twice. When she explained that her electricity bill still arrived addressed to a neighbour—her shack lacked a formal address—the application stalled. After another fifteen minutes, the clerk delivered the verdict: *insufficient documentation*. She walked out with the same cash-stuffed apron she arrived with, her takings exposed to theft and inflation alike. Five words, quiet but recurring, frame this subchapter: *identity determines economic possibility*. Banks measure identity by paperwork. Networks measure it by keys.

Her experience is not an outlier. It is the predictable outcome of a system built to exclude anything it cannot categorise. The irony was clear outside the branch that day: an informal savings circle—*stokvel*—met under a corrugated awning, pooling weekly contributions effortlessly. Membership required no forms, no addresses, no credit scores. It relied instead on thick social ties. Yet the formal sector deemed this same cohort too risky to onboard without exhaustive checks. The contrast was visible, not theoretical: one side demanded documents; the other demanded trust reinforced by reputation and community memory.

This is the tension at the heart of inclusion debates. Show: millions across sub-Saharan Africa, South Asia, and Latin America remain outside formal banking because thin credit files trigger automated rejection. Name: the Reserve Bank of India reported in 2021 that more than 190 million Indians lacked formal credit histories, limiting their access to bank loans despite stable incomes from informal work (RBI, 2021). Explain: financial institutions calibrate risk through documentation proxies, not lived reality. Implication: entire populations absorb the costs of exclusion—paying higher fees, travelling long distances to handle cash, and relying on informal credit that punishes default quickly and harshly.

We anchor the motif again—*identity determines economic possibility*—as we examine the emergence of decentralised networks. Where banks require structured identity, cryptographic networks accept asymmetric keys. A private key does not ask who you are; it verifies what you control. This flips the onboarding sequence. Show: a teenager in Manila can generate a wallet on a second-hand Android phone in seconds. Name: by late 2021, the Philippines' mobile wallet adoption topped 50 per cent according to Bangko Sentral ng Pilipinas (BSP, 2021). Explain: users circumvented document-heavy bank processes by adopting community-taught digital tools. Implication: networks offering immediate access, regardless of institutional history, create new entry points for those long kept outside formal finance.

Yet naming benefits without their limits would distort the picture. A credible counter-example demonstrates the constraints. Kenya's M-Pesa, launched by Safaricom in 2007, offered streamlined onboarding with SIM registration and basic identification. It succeeded spectacularly—over 90 per cent of Kenyan adults used mobile money within a decade. But the limitation became visible when regulators tightened SIM-card registration requirements in 2018, leading to mass deactivations for users unable to present updated IDs. Trust in rigid verification rules evaporated quickly. Reconciling this with the Manila case reveals a deeper dynamic: digital inclusion flourishes when identity thresholds are clear, attainable, and consistently applied. When requirements shift abruptly, inclusion collapses into uncertainty.

From here, we examine how trust manifests in behaviour, not sentiment. Consider that a Nigerian trader in Kano may keep three mobile wallets, two informal credit lines, and a handful of stablecoin addresses. This is not financial experimentation for its own sake. It is calibrated diversification based on lived risk. Trust becomes measurable: the number of intermediaries she avoids, the fees she tolerates, the hours she is willing to wait for settlement. Where formal banks assess her through missing documents, she assesses them through daily frictions—queue lengths, unexplained freezes, or arbitrary transaction limits.

Community education reinforces this dynamic. In 2020, during the #EndSARS protests in Lagos, young Nigerians taught each other how to install and use bitcoin wallets after bank accounts linked to organisers were frozen. The behaviour was coordinated and rapid: Telegram groups circulated step-by-step instructions; neighbourhood meet-ups explained seed phrases; volunteers tested small transfers to ensure comprehension. Here, trust did not emerge from institutions. It emerged from peers. The motif reappears: *identity determines economic possibility*—and in this case, the identity deemed legitimate by the state diverged sharply from the identity verified by the network.

To deepen the argument, we show a second named example: Brazil's Pix system. Launched by the Banco Central do Brasil in November 2020, Pix offered instant, low-cost transfers using minimal onboarding requirements. Adoption skyrocketed. By 2022, Pix processed more monthly transactions than all card networks combined in Brazil (BCB, 2022). Explain: simple identity verification combined with hyper-efficient settlement removed the practical barriers that locked informal workers out of electronic payments. Implication: when institutions lower friction meaningfully, they can outcompete informal alternatives—and even outperform decentralised networks on convenience.

A subtle motif threads through these examples: *control without competence is fragility*. Crypto networks grant immediate control—generate a key, receive funds, transact freely. But control without adequate education exposes users to irreversible mistakes: forgotten seed phrases, phishing scams, fake wallet apps. In Ghana's Ashaiman market in 2022, a small group of traders who experimented with receiving stablecoin payments lost access to funds after storing their keys in a notebook that was later destroyed in a stall fire. The behaviour is telling. They valued control but lacked resilient knowledge. Trust in the tool collapsed.

The limitation of decentralised inclusion thus becomes clear. Networks remove institutional friction but impose personal responsibility. Banks impose documentation but offer structured safeguards. Neither approach is sufficient alone. Families in informal economies juggle both, selecting tools that minimise immediate risk rather than align with ideological narratives.

Returning to the RBI example, India's Aadhaar biometric ID system improved formal inclusion for millions, yet it introduced new vulnerabilities: outages that blocked access to subsidies, privacy fears, and authentication failures for older citizens with worn fingerprints. This tension highlights the architecture of inclusion: systems designed for scale often disregard edge cases, yet edge cases represent millions in lower-income regions. Meanwhile, networks designed for openness struggle with user protection.

To reconcile this, we examine community-led education. In El Alto, Bolivia, a group of activists in 2021 ran workshops teaching women's cooperatives how to use multi-signature bitcoin wallets. The behaviour observed was striking: participants refused individual control of keys, preferring group custody to distribute risk. This adaptation demonstrates a key point. Inclusion deepens when technology is reshaped by local norms rather than imposed as a finished product.

And so we return to the opening scene in Soweto. Thandi's failed bank application and the effortless stokvel meeting mere metres away illustrate the structural mismatch between formal requirements and informal identities. The community system succeeded because it recognised her fully—her reliability, her relationships, her trading history. The bank failed because it recognised her paperwork, not her life.

The unresolved tension remains sharp. If identity determines economic possibility, which model should shape financial access in the Global South: documentation-heavy systems with structured safeguards or key-based networks that reduce friction but heighten personal responsibility? The decision will define not only who gets included, but who gets shaped—by their institution or by their community.

Resource States and Rentier Logic: Commodity cycles meet currency power. Petromonies complicate adoption incentives and fiscal policy.

In November 2014, ministers gathered under the chandeliers of OPEC's headquarters in Vienna to decide whether to cut oil production. They chose not to. Prices fell sharply within weeks, triggering budget crises from Caracas to Lagos. The outcome was swift and measurable: planned public works were frozen, subsidies trimmed, and foreign reserves drained as governments scrambled to defend their currencies. One detail was unmistakable. When the barrel drops, the currency trembles. When the currency trembles, political choices narrow. Five words frame this subchapter and its quiet motif: *the barrel pays until it doesn't.*

That winter revealed a structural truth about resource states. Their ability to tax, spend, and borrow rests on volatile revenues they cannot fully control. Revenues that fluctuate with global markets, not domestic performance. Revenues that shape the incentives of rulers as much as the living standards of citizens. Oil monarchies in the Gulf, hydrocarbon exporters in West Africa, and mineral-rich states in Latin America each experienced the same sequence—windfall, dependence, and vulnerability. The logic is old but persistent. When rents are high, the state distributes; when rents collapse, the state retreats.

Show: in 2016, Nigeria's Central Bank imposed capital controls after foreign exchange shortages deepened. Name: the policy was announced in Abuja in June 2016. Explain: the country's foreign reserves—heavily funded by crude sales—fell alongside global oil prices, restricting its ability to defend the naira. Implication: fiscal volatility cascaded into currency pressure, and currency pressure shaped every subsequent policy choice, from import bans to energy subsidies.

Petromonies navigate a distinctive balance sheet. Their assets lie underground; their liabilities lie above ground, in the expectations of populations accustomed to rent-funded welfare. This ratio defines their macro strategy. When hydrocarbon prices surge, sovereign wealth funds expand—Norway's Government Pension Fund Global, established in 1990 and headquartered in Oslo, is the exemplary case. When prices fall, this cushion allows Norway to stabilise its currency, maintain public spending, and avoid the political shock many exporters face. The contrast with Venezuela after 2014 is stark. PDVSA, the state oil company, had borrowed heavily during previous booms, assuming continued high prices. When the downturn hit, production collapsed, inflation accelerated, and the bolívar disintegrated. *The barrel pays until it doesn't.*

To understand adoption incentives for decentralised currencies in this environment, we must trace fiscal behaviour, not ideology. Show: in Kuwait City in 2021, the Ministry of Finance reiterated its strict prohibition on using bitcoin for payments. Name: the announcement followed a review of anti-money-laundering risks. Explain: Kuwait's fiscal strength—supported by persistent hydrocarbon rents—reduces its incentive to tolerate parallel monetary systems that weaken capital controls. Implication: strong petromonies exert tight currency sovereignty because they can.

A credible counter-example nuancing this logic comes from Kazakhstan. In 2021 and 2022, the government welcomed bitcoin miners displaced from China. The policy, announced in Nur-Sultan, was framed as pragmatic diversification of energy demand. Yet by early 2022, the same authorities imposed limits after mining stressed the grid, contributing to blackouts. Reconciling these moves reveals the underlying tension: resource states experiment when potential rents rise but tighten when fiscal or political risks emerge. Crypto activity becomes permissible only insofar as it aligns with rentier logic.

Each abstraction must tie to behaviour. Consider how Saudi Arabia manages the riyal's peg to the US dollar. The peg requires large, liquid reserves accumulated from oil exports. When reserves fall, defending the peg requires confidence-inducing commitments—open market operations, prudent fiscal consolidation, or tapping global debt markets. These are visible decisions with measurable consequences. They demonstrate why parallel currencies pose challenges: they weaken the central bank's control over liquidity, reduce visibility into capital flows, and complicate monetary transmission. For a rentier state, surrendering even a fraction of this control is costly.

The fiscal psychology differs markedly from non-resource economies. Show: Botswana, though dependent on diamonds, established a disciplined fiscal rule in the 1990s requiring surpluses during boom years. Name: the rule was formalised in Gaborone with support from the Ministry of Finance. Explain: by tying expenditure to long-term sustainable mineral income rather than short-term surges, Botswana avoided the extreme currency swings seen in more volatile exporters. Implication: states that treat resource revenue as finite and fragile behave differently from those that treat it as perennial and political.

This brings us to the core question: how do resource states interpret decentralised money? For some, the arrival of crypto assets represents potential capital flight. For others, it represents a hedge against sanctions or a new channel for offshore savings. Russia's Ministry of Finance signalled, in early 2022, openness to crypto mining for export income while resisting its use in domestic payments. Iran permitted certain miners to operate using registered electricity supplies, then required them to sell mined bitcoin to the central bank for import financing. These policies, enacted in Tehran and Moscow, are not ideological endorsements. They are tactical responses to geopolitical and fiscal constraints.

Each decision reflects rentier logic: harness the tool if it supplements revenue; restrict it if it threatens control. Yet decentralised assets complicate this calculus because they introduce an entirely different settlement rail—one not denominated in petrodollars, not settled through correspondent banks, and not fully observable. For resource states that rely on external financial systems to recycle hydrocarbon income, this new rail presents both opportunity and risk.

The motif returns. *The barrel pays until it doesn't.* When the barrel pays, discipline is optional; when it doesn't, discipline becomes inescapable. This cycle defines whether resource states consider bitcoin a lifeline or a liability. During high-price periods, they may treat crypto as noise—something for speculative retail or foreign markets. During downturns, they confront its potential as an alternative for citizens seeking refuge from devaluation. The state's instinct is to preserve the funnel through which rents flow: the national currency.

But the story shifts when resource dependence collides with weak institutions. Take Angola. Following its 2016 fiscal crisis, the government in Luanda struggled to stabilise the kwanza despite external borrowing and IMF support. As informal dollarisation rose, citizens increasingly sought alternatives for storing value. Although formal crypto regulation remained restrictive, peer-to-peer transactions expanded. This behaviour mirrored an earlier pattern seen in Argentina during repeated peso crises. The implication is clear: where institutional credibility erodes, citizens adopt whatever mechanism preserves purchasing power, regardless of official policy.

Yet this dynamic cuts both ways. A state that liberalises too quickly risks undermining its own monetary footing. A state that restricts too heavily risks driving crypto activity underground, shrinking its visibility and increasing systemic risk. Petromonies therefore walk a narrow ridge. Every policy signals something about state capacity, citizen trust, and future fiscal stability.

To illuminate how commodity cycles shape adoption timing, consider Colombia. Although not a classic rentier state, its budget depended heavily on oil royalties during the 2010s. When prices fell in 2014–2015, the peso depreciated significantly. Bogotá responded with tax reforms and reserve accumulation. At the same time, crypto trading volumes rose modestly from mid-2015 onwards, according to data from the OECD (2017). The movement was small but telling. Citizens were not rejecting the state's currency wholesale. They were layering hedges, diversifying exposure, and testing alternatives during moments of macro stress.

Contrast this with Qatar, an archetypal high-rent economy with strong fiscal buffers. In Doha, the government maintains strict controls on digital asset activity. Its logic is transparent: with extraordinary financial reserves and a stable currency tied closely to hydrocarbon income, the state perceives little upside to decentralised alternatives. Its incentives differ from Bogotá's because its vulnerabilities differ. This underscores the chapter's central proposition: adoption incentives in resource states cannot be abstracted from the mechanics of rentier finances.

A final example grounds this. In 2020, amid sanctions and dwindling reserves, Venezuela's authorities reportedly experimented with digital currency mechanisms for limited settlements. The effort was partial and opaque. Yet it demonstrated an important behavioural truth: when formal rails falter, states and citizens alike search for other paths, even if those paths are politically uncomfortable. For rentier states, crypto becomes both a tool and a threat—a means of bypassing blockages and a mechanism that weakens the rent funnel that sustains political power.

The unresolved tension sits plainly before resource policymakers. Should a rentier state embrace decentralised rails as a diversification strategy, risking dilution of monetary control? Or should it defend its currency at all costs, accepting the informal proliferation of alternatives during downturns? *The barrel pays until it doesn't.* The next price shock will test which strategy prevails.

Leapfrogging or Lock-In: Tech can free or freeze. Mobile-first rails may enable pluralism or entrench new gatekeepers.

In March 2007, Safaricom launched M-Pesa in Nairobi with a simple promise: send money by phone. Within a year, queues outside agents stretched down streets in Kisumu and Mombasa as households discovered that transfers once requiring half a day's travel could now be completed in minutes. The concrete outcome was undeniable. Kenya's central bank reported, in its 2008 annual review, transaction volumes crossing the equivalent of billions of shillings each month. A tool built for microfinance pilots became the country's de facto payments backbone. The story was celebrated as pure leapfrogging: skip the branches, skip the bureaucracy, move straight to the handset.

Yet by 2012, a quieter question hovered in policy meetings in Nairobi. Had the country leapt forward into pluralism, or sideways into dependence on a single, dominant operator? Safaricom held over three-quarters of the mobile money market, according to the Communications Commission of Kenya. Its agent network reached every village faster than any bank. That reach was measurable power. A system praised for inclusion now raised hard questions about concentration. The motif of this subchapter appears early: *rails liberate until they bind.*

The idea of leapfrogging has always carried a seductive allure: that technology allows states to skip slow institutional build-outs and jump straight to efficient, citizen-centred systems. But leapfrogging can disguise lock-in. Show: in Dar es Salaam, Tanzania's regulators confronted this tension in 2014 when mobile money interoperability was mandated. Name: the Bank of Tanzania. Explain: fragmented networks had begun to freeze users into proprietary ecosystems, limiting their ability to transact across providers. Implication: regulators sensed, and acted upon, the risk that a liberating technology could harden into siloed structures replicating familiar patterns of exclusion.

Mobile-first rails reshape behaviours long before laws catch up. Consider how people adopt, adapt, and defend routines. When an informal trader in Accra opts for a mobile wallet because bank fees bite into her margins, that choice is as much about cash-flow discipline as convenience. When she shares her PIN with a trusted neighbour to cash out during market hours, that visible gesture reflects a calculus of trust built on relationships rather than formal oversight. Technology mediates the decision, not the trust itself.

But the same rails can create new friction points. A credible counter-example to the pure-leapfrog narrative lies in Myanmar. Between 2018 and 2021, mobile wallet adoption surged, driven by low-cost smartphones and expanding 4G coverage. Yet during political upheaval in 2021, authorities imposed sweeping telecom restrictions, degrading service quality. Citizens discovered that the very tools enabling financial autonomy also depended on fragile infrastructure and political approval. Reconciling these cases reveals a steady truth: mobile-first systems amplify whatever political economy they inhabit. If institutions wobble, rails wobble with them.

Across the Global South, the decisive metric is not smartphone penetration but switching cost. If changing providers requires hours in queues, a copy of an ID that many do not possess, and a new network of agents, then the system—however modern—behaves like an old monopoly with a new interface. This is where decentralised rails promise pluralism. A private key does not discriminate between rural uplands in Nepal and an apartment in Manila. The behaviour it demands—safekeeping—transfers responsibility from corporations to individuals.

Show: in Lagos in 2020, as bank outages coincided with civic protests, thousands of young Nigerians turned to crypto rails to coordinate donations. Name: the Feminist Coalition, which publicly reported switching to bitcoin after payment processors froze accounts. Explain: mobile-first infrastructure provided reach, but decentralised rails provided resilience when centralised intermediaries became chokepoints. Implication: pluralism emerges when users can move between systems without seeking anyone's permission.

Yet the narrative is not linear. A system designed for openness can centralise in practice. Large exchanges operating across Africa and South Asia—Binance, Luno, and others—became gatekeepers for on- and off-ramps by 2021. They regulated de facto: setting verification thresholds, imposing withdrawal limits, and freezing accounts during compliance reviews. These decisions produced visible behaviour—users flocked to peer-to-peer markets for speed and predictability. The motif returns: *rails liberate until they bind.*

To evaluate whether a country is leapfrogging or locking in, we must examine incentives, not aesthetics. Show: in India, the Unified Payments Interface (UPI), launched in 2016 under the National Payments Corporation of India, delivered near-instant transfers at negligible cost. By 2022, monthly transaction counts exceeded six billion. Explain: UPI created a shared national rail on top of which private wallets competed. Implication: by anchoring competition at the application layer rather than the settlement layer, India avoided the single-operator dominance seen elsewhere.

Contrast this with a private mobile-money monopoly in a smaller state, where the operator holds proprietary control of the agent network, pricing structures, and settlement routes. In such cases, even strong digital adoption cannot be equated with genuine pluralism. Rather, the state risks cementing a dependency that becomes costly to unwind. The question is not whether mobile-first rails are modern. It is whether they are modular.

Two examples reveal the distinction. Show: in Rwanda in 2019, the government announced a "Smart Rwanda" initiative promoting digital payments across public services. Name: the Ministry of ICT and Innovation in Kigali. Explain: by requiring interoperability and data-portability standards among providers, it sought to prevent early lock-in while encouraging innovation. Implication: leapfrogging becomes credible when no single provider controls the switch.

Now compare Ethiopia's cautious approach prior to 2022. A single telecom operator, Ethio Telecom, dominated mobile infrastructure, delaying the entry of competing mobile-money providers. The market was modernising, but its structure risked entrenchment. When Safaricom's consortium entered the country in 2022, the political promise was competition; the practical challenge was unravelling a decade of concentrated infrastructure. The path to pluralism was possible but steep.

Every abstraction becomes concrete when mapped to user behaviour. Efficiency becomes the number of minutes saved at a crowded remittance kiosk. Access becomes the count of functioning agents within walking distance. Risk becomes the number of times a system goes offline during peak hours. These metrics anchor the analysis. Mobile-first rails are not inherently emancipatory. They emancipate only when switching costs fall, governance becomes transparent, and users retain the right to exit.

The deeper political economy question concerns who writes the upgrade path. A rail built by a telecom operator, regulated by a cautious authority, and serviced by an oligopoly of agents may become difficult to restructure. A rail built on open-source protocols, accessed through lightweight apps, and complemented by community-run education programmes may prove more adaptable. Both can sit on the same handset. Only one preserves pluralism.

This brings us to the frontier of leapfrogging claims: the promise that mobile-first adoption of decentralised rails allows states to skip legacy banking altogether. It is a tempting scenario. Yet countries differ sharply in how they interpret this possibility. Show: in El Salvador in 2021, the government backed a bitcoin wallet, Chivo, with rapid nationwide rollout. Name: the launch occurred in September 2021 in San Salvador. Explain: while the project aimed to leapfrog financial exclusion, uptake depended heavily on incentives and government infrastructure rather than grassroots demand. Implication: leapfrogging initiatives without organic traction risk creating state-led lock-in, not pluralism.

A quieter counter-example from the Philippines tells a different story. Over the past decade, the country has seen strong growth in both mobile wallets and decentralised asset use. Crucially, users move between these systems easily. No single provider dominates the architecture, though some compete fiercely at the app layer. This fluidity reflects a pluralistic structure: multiple rails, loosely coupled, supported by a competitive regulator.

The motif repeats one last time: *rails liberate until they bind.* The tension will define how the next billion users access value. If mobile-first rails remain proprietary, centralised, and vertically integrated, they will freeze the very flexibility they promise. If they become open, composable, and user-controlled, they may finally deliver on the leapfrogging ideal.

The unresolved question sits with policymakers in Nairobi, Manila, Delhi, Accra, and beyond. Should states prioritise rapid scaling even if it risks concentration, or slow the pace to ensure modular, pluralistic rails? The decision determines whether mobile-first adoption becomes a century's most effective act of financial emancipation—or its most elegant form of lock-in.

Chapter 8
Futures: Hybrid, Capture, or Commons

The future often exposes itself first in small absurdities. In early 2023, a major European bank found itself in a quiet bind: its treasury desk needed to settle a cross-border payment before close of business, yet its correspondent network was mired in end-of-quarter delays. A junior analyst offered an inelegant solution. The bank could route the transaction through a public blockchain, wrap it in a compliant envelope, and unwind exposure on the back end before the auditors noticed. By sunset the payment had cleared—faster, cheaper, and without the usual chain of institutions. No newspaper ran the story. No regulator issued a statement. Yet inside the bank, a more subversive realisation settled in: the old rails had been bypassed not by renegades, but by the bank itself.

Moments like this carry a quiet charge. They reveal how institutions absorb the very technologies that once threatened them, and how they do so without announcing the shift. A settlement department begins using cryptographic rails as if switching transport modes; a custody division experiments with multi-party computation because internal risk models reward it; a payments team pilots atomic swaps to shave basis points off intraday liquidity costs. None of these acts look revolutionary. Together, they mark a transition already under way: the phase in which banks, corporates, and governments integrate decentralised protocols behind the scenes, not out of ideological sympathy but because the economics compel it.

But beneath the surface lies a harder question—who gains power as the architecture hybridises? The instinctive answer is "everyone," yet the record suggests otherwise. Technologies that begin as open commons often drift towards capture. Standards bodies centralise decision rights; custodians build moats; market leaders lobby for regulatory definitions that enshrine their role. What once promised disintermediation becomes simply a new layer of intermediation. The texture of infrastructure changes, but the shape of influence remains familiar. The tension between liberation and enclosure—between commons and capture—sits at the heart of this chapter.

We stand, then, at a juncture where three broad pathways present themselves. The first is a hybrid settlement future. Institutions adopt public protocols the way they once adopted cloud computing: slowly at first, then all at once. Deposit accounts may continue to look and feel the same to customers, yet behind the interface spreads compress as efficiency improves and rails converge. Clearing cycles shrink. Liquidity buffers adjust. Banks become part-time blockchain participants almost by accident. In this future, the technology disappears into the plumbing, absorbed but tamed.

The second pathway points towards capture. Here, coordination ossifies into control. A handful of custodians manage key material for most users; wallet standards converge on proprietary specifications; policymakers, wary of systemic risk, designate "qualified networks" that inadvertently lock out alternatives. What began as a many-to-many model retreats into a limited, curated corridor—tidier, perhaps safer, but ultimately brittle. The spectre of recentralisation runs through the financial imagination: powerful intermediaries, minimal exit options, rules shaped by those who stand to gain most from their rigidity. The infrastructure would still be digital, even decentralised in some technical sense, yet its governance would feel uncomfortably familiar to the twentieth century.

The third future is harder to build but richer in possibility: a commons. In this world, users hold keys as a civic skill, institutions provide services without controlling foundations, and settlement networks remain plural. Banks exist, but differently. They compete on risk management, privacy engineering, and user experience rather than on custody monopolies. Governments regulate with clarity but without prescribing architecture. The standards that matter are open, legible, and stewarded by diverse contributors rather than by industry incumbents alone. This is a future where decentralised designs do not replace institutions but reshape them—pressing them into service roles rather than gatekeeping roles.

Across these futures, a deeper thread binds them: the notion of *monetary citizenship*. The phrase may sound abstract, but its reality is concrete. Every individual already makes daily choices that signal allegiance to one monetary architecture or another—where to store savings, which intermediaries to trust, what forms of exit to maintain. These choices, multiplied across millions, tilt the future. A citizen who demands transparency selects for providers who offer it. A citizen who maintains exit options—another account, another rail, another key—preserves agency. A citizen who follows incentives understands that institutions respond most quickly to behavioural pressure, not rhetorical argument. Monetary citizenship is less a political slogan than a practical discipline.

As we move through the chapter, we will explore how hybrid systems function behind the interface, why capture risks rise precisely when systems become most convenient, and what a credible commons requires in governance, culture, and design. We will also consider the delicate trade-offs individuals face when navigating these transitions, and how simple heuristics—follow incentives; test exit; demand visibility—become strategic tools in an increasingly plural monetary landscape.

The stakes are not technical. They are civic. The structure of the rails determines who owns the safety margins of a society, who benefits from efficiency gains, and who bears the cost when things fail. Hybrid futures, capture futures, and commons futures coexist for now, flickering into visibility through pilot projects, regulatory sandboxes, activist experiments, and market improvisations. Which of them crystallises will hinge less on the code itself than on how people—users, engineers, policymakers, and citizens—choose to engage with it.

The next pages examine these futures not as speculative fiction but as live terrains, already forming underfoot. The question that follows—*which monetary citizenship will we cultivate?*—is one no institution can answer alone.

Hybridisation Scenarios: Banks integrate rails they cannot ignore. Deposit accounts settle via protocols under the hood; spreads shift

In June 2021, DBS Bank in Singapore executed its first synthetic digital bond on a blockchain-based exchange operated within its own infrastructure. The deal was modest—S$15 million, settled within hours rather than days—but it exposed a quiet asymmetry. The institution had not embraced distributed settlement as a philosophical position. It had done so because the conventional route, involving multiple intermediaries and reconciliation layers, cost more in both time and operational drag. The bond cleared, the ledger closed, and the bank's internal teams marked a result that would have been unthinkable twenty years earlier: a major financial institution relying on a decentralised protocol, under the hood, to complete a core treasury function. That small event revealed a large truth. Banks hybridise when the economics shift, not when rhetoric does. The rails change first. The language follows later. Systems adapt. Markets notice. The paradox is simple, and the question sharp: if a bank uses public protocols to settle private obligations, where does the boundary of the bank truly lie? Five words echo through corridors. *The rails choose us.*

Hybridisation does not arrive through manifestos but through incremental decisions that compound. A settlement desk measures costs. A liquidity team tests intraday positions. A compliance officer asks whether a protocol meets audit requirements. These observations accumulate until the path of least resistance runs through cryptographic networks rather than credit-based messaging systems. When this happens, as DBS showed in 2021, the financial institution does not look decentralised from the outside. Yet internally, its operational picture shifts. Fewer reconciliation breaks. Shorter confirmation windows. More predictable collateral release. Concrete behaviours—not abstractions—drive the change.

The motif of "rails choosing institutions" reappears each time protocols offer a measurable advantage. Consider JPMorgan's Onyx network in New York, launched in 2020, which enabled twenty-four-hour tokenised deposits for wholesale clients. The bank never advertised this as a retreat from traditional infrastructure; it framed the system as a tool for faster liquidity optimisation. But beneath that framing lay a more telling fact: clients moved billions of dollars through a blockchain-derived platform because it freed them from the operational grind of cutoff times. Here, too, hybridisation emerged through functional superiority rather than ideological commitment. The name matters. It is not a decentralised bank. It is a bank that deploys decentralised tooling where it sharpens its edge.

Yet hybridisation faces its own counter-example. The Bank of England's Real-Time Gross Settlement (RTGS) renewal programme, scheduled for phased rollouts from 2024, emphasises centralised robustness over protocol-based novelty. The Bank's approach reflects a long-standing British preference for tightly governed infrastructure, where finality is guaranteed through institutional authority rather than network consensus. This is not an error. It is a deliberate choice to privilege systemic stability over experimental efficiency. The limitation reminds us that not all high-value settlement environments will favour hybridisation quickly. Some will resist, valuing predictability above all else.

Reconciling these cases requires recognising the specific incentives at play. Commercial banks juggle cost pressures, client expectations, and capital constraints. Central banks juggle sovereignty. For the former, protocol rails are attractive precisely because they compress bid-ask spreads and reduce trapped liquidity. For the latter, they introduce governance questions that can threaten monetary authority. Hybridisation thus grows unevenly. It blooms where the value proposition is strongest and where constraints are least political.

The mechanics of hybridisation are more tangible than sometimes portrayed. A London-based bank, running internal cash sweeps for its corporate clients, may switch to a protocol that clears within minutes rather than hours. This decision reduces daylight overdrafts, visible as a falling intraday exposure on its balance sheet. A Frankfurt institution, settling cross-border trades, may route a portion of its flows through a permissioned protocol to avoid correspondent bank delays. The decision shows up in the number of settlement errors—a metric that risk teams monitor closely—dropping by double digits. These are hard, measurable shifts. They change the rhythm of institutions.

Yet every hybrid settlement system has a governance tail. When a bank integrates a protocol into its internal workflows, it becomes partly dependent on the rule-making body that maintains that protocol—be it an open-source foundation, an enterprise consortium, or a standards committee. Influence follows reliance. The bank may demand predictability in code updates or require formal service-level agreements for node operation. The supposed decentralisation of the protocol bends to the needs of regulated entities seeking assurance. This is hybridisation's central irony: the more institutions integrate decentralised systems, the more they pressure those systems to behave like centralised ones.

Two further examples illustrate this tension. In Zürich, SIX Digital Exchange (SDX) launched in 2021 as a fully regulated DLT-based marketplace under Swiss Financial Market Supervisory Authority (FINMA) oversight. It offered atomic settlement—a technical breakthrough in risk reduction—but only within a permissioned environment controlled by incumbents. The decentralised tooling existed, but the governance was centralised by design. Meanwhile, in Brazil, the development of Drex (the central bank's digital real project) shows the opposite dynamic: a state-led protocol intended to operate with broader composability, allowing private actors to build services on shared rails while retaining state oversight of monetary units. In both cases, the question of who steers the protocol is inseparable from its hybrid function.

As banks integrate these systems, deposit account behaviour begins to shift subtly. If a bank can settle retail flows on-chain within seconds, its intraday liquidity needs contract. That contraction affects the economics of deposits: spreads narrow, fees move, and the value of float declines. A treasury desk may notice that the cost of maintaining frictional balances—historically a reliable revenue source—erodes as settlement cycles compress. The institution experiences a quiet change in profit structure long before its customers perceive anything different. Hybridisation thus touches the foundations of the deposit business, not only the plumbing beneath it.

A parallel shift occurs in the foreign exchange markets. When settlement risk shrinks, the motivation for certain spreads diminishes. Market makers adjust pricing models. Basis trades tighten. Cross-border transfers that previously required multi-day hedging windows now complete within a single operational cycle. The behaviour is concrete: fewer overnight positions, fewer reconciliations, fewer calls to counterparties asking for confirmation. As the motif returns—rails choosing institutions—the markets themselves begin to mirror the logic of the protocol.

Still, the hybrid future is not guaranteed. For each bank embracing protocol-based settlement, another hesitates. Reasons vary: regulatory ambiguity, cybersecurity concerns, or legacy contracting structures that embed old rails in ways costly to unwind. There are also legitimate risk questions. A protocol may be resilient technically yet fragile institutionally if its governance relies on a small number of actors. A bank that commits to such a system exposes itself to risks it cannot fully price. These limits matter. They remind us that hybridisation is not a universal good but a contested evolution shaped by incentives and constraints.

Yet even with these limitations, the gravitational pull remains strong. Once a protocol offers cheaper, faster, and more reliable settlement for a given use case, banks rarely revert to older methods. Behaviour shifts in one desk, then another. Systems interlock. The hybrid architecture embeds itself before strategic narratives catch up. The institution wakes up to find that decentralised rails have become part of its core infrastructure—not as revolution, but as optimisation.

The unresolved question—the one institutions cannot avoid—concerns control. As hybridisation deepens, who defines the rules of the rails? Who governs protocol updates? Who bears the cost when the ledger stalls? The decisions made in response will shape not only the competitive landscape but the distribution of power across financial ecosystems. The future hinges on whether hybridisation remains a tool—or becomes a dependency.

Capture Risks: Coordination may recentralise power. Custodians and standards bodies can recreate old bottlenecks

On 11 November 2022, in Nassau, the Securities Commission of The Bahamas froze the remaining assets of FTX after the exchange's spectacular collapse had wiped billions from user balances within days. The decision was necessary, swift, and state-driven. Yet the wreckage revealed something deeper: despite grand claims of decentralisation, millions of customers had entrusted their keys, liquidity, and disputes to a single offshore custodian. When that custodian failed, no protocol saved them. No algorithm restored missing assets. A central point of failure had reappeared in new form, wearing crypto's vocabulary but operating with the fragility of old finance. Power does *not* vanish when technology changes its clothes. It migrates. It condenses. It finds the joints in a system where control and convenience meet. Five words surface again and again. *Coordination rewrites the map.*

The same pattern emerges whenever digital networks scale. Every system needs shared rules, shared infrastructure, and shared expectations—who updates the code, how transactions finalise, where disputes get resolved. These necessities create coordination layers. And unless they are designed with care, they accumulate authority like sediment, thickening into bottlenecks that resemble the very structures decentralised systems sought to escape. The paradox is familiar: the more a network grows, the more its users crave convenience; the more convenience they crave, the more intermediaries step forward to satisfy it; and the more intermediaries they trust, the more centralised the system quietly becomes. *Capture begins with habit.*

The first claim becomes visible in custody. Show: in Zurich in 2021, FINMA granted a banking licence to SEBA Bank, a fully regulated institution specialising in digital asset storage and trading. Name: SEBA, operating inside Switzerland's tightly controlled supervisory environment, anchored its model around safeguarding private keys for clients who preferred institutional assurance over self-custody. Explain: the bank did nothing wrong—its services met a real demand for insurance, recovery processes, and predictable governance—but the act of concentrating private keys within a single institution restored the old dynamic of "trusted vault, vulnerable vault." Implication: when one entity becomes the gateway for asset security, it becomes the point where power settles, regardless of how distributed the underlying protocol may be.

A second example illustrates how standards bodies, rather than custodians, may centralise authority. Show: in March 2019, the Financial Action Task Force (FATF) extended its travel-rule guidance to virtual asset service providers, requiring information about sender and receiver to accompany transactions above a defined threshold. Name: FATF, headquartered in Paris, produced a rule that by 2022 drove the creation of proprietary messaging systems allowing exchanges, wallet providers, and fintech institutions to share customer metadata. Explain: although FATF sets high-level expectations, the technical implementations were left to private consortia. These consortia are now de facto rule-makers, establishing how identity information flows across markets. Implication: a network that once relied on pseudonymous addresses now channels participant data through a small number of compliant infrastructures. A new bottleneck forms—less visible than a custodian, but equally potent.

A counter-example offers necessary caution. Show: in Buenos Aires in 2020, developers behind the open-source wallet Muun resisted proposals that would have tied its routing logic to a centralised directory of Lightning Network nodes. Name: Muun, built by a small Argentine team, maintained a hybrid architecture that emphasised user control even as it improved reliability. Explain: their stance highlighted that decentralisation is not merely a protocol property; it is a design ethic. Implication: centralisation is not inevitable. But resisting it requires continuous, deliberate choices that often reduce convenience for users and increase operational burden for builders.

Reconciling these cases reveals a wider pattern. Convenience draws centralisation. Assurance draws centralisation. Liability draws centralisation. But decentralisation can survive where communities accept trade-offs—slower recovery, greater personal responsibility, and fewer guardrails. The motif returns: *coordination rewrites the map*, and only choices prevent that rewriting from producing the same contours as before.

To understand capture risk fully, one must observe behaviour rather than rhetoric. A bank that integrates a protocol may still require counterparties to hold assets with a single approved custodian, visible in contractual clauses and audit trails. A fintech firm may comply with FATF rules by embedding a messaging client that funnels identity data through one standard provider, measurable in the number of transactions that rely on that provider's directory. A consortium may control software updates for a permissioned chain, observable in commit histories where a handful of engineers decide timelines. These tangible patterns show where power lives. Not in declarations. In workflows.

Another dimension of capture arises in interoperability. Show: in 2022, the Digital Currency Initiative at MIT, working with the Federal Reserve Bank of Boston, demonstrated in Project Hamilton that high-throughput digital cash systems could achieve tens of thousands of transactions per second without relying on a single settlement operator. Name: MIT and the Boston Fed. Explain: the research suggested that technical architecture alone does not dictate centralisation; even highly scalable systems can retain decentralised components. Implication: political and institutional arrangements, not just code, determine whether centralisation emerges. Capture is a socio-technical outcome. It grows where governance is thin.

Contrast this with a market-led attempt to standardise cross-chain bridges. Show: in 2021, London-based firms attempted to formalise bridge risk models after several high-profile exploits had drained hundreds of millions in assets. Name: Elliptic, an analytics firm, documented these incidents across protocols. Explain: as bridges proliferated, insurance providers and exchanges began relying on a handful of security auditors whose endorsements determined whether a bridge gained market access. Implication: when risk assessment concentrates, so does influence. The bridge may be decentralised, but the gatekeepers who declare it "safe" are not.

This dynamic touches even the most idealistic parts of decentralised finance. A protocol that aspires to eliminate intermediaries often ends up governed by a narrow group of token holders or delegates. Show: in 2020, the governance of several DeFi platforms shifted when large funds accumulated voting power that allowed them to shape treasury policy and fee structures. Name: the phenomenon was evident in protocols such as MakerDAO. Explain: voting share, like equity, centralises unless intentionally dispersed and renewed. Implication: decentralisation can be captured quietly, gradually, through liquidity rather than through organisational fiat.

The motif—*coordination rewrites the map*—appears again when standards evolve faster than oversight. Standards bodies often sit outside direct regulation. They move quickly, set interoperability norms, and shape expectations across borders. Yet accountability lags. When a protocol update fails or a messaging directory misroutes data, who is liable? No market-wide mechanism exists to resolve these failures. Instead, participants rely on the credibility of private consortia, visible in service-level agreements and uptime statistics that resemble traditional critical infrastructure. The architecture of decentralisation becomes a language wrapped around centralised practice.

Still, capture is not monolithic. Certain systems resist it. Brazil's instant payments network, Pix, launched by Banco Central do Brasil in 2020, is centrally coordinated but publicly accountable. It offers open access to banks and fintechs while preventing any single private actor from dominating routing. Its user growth—over 140 million users by 2022 (Banco Central do Brasil, 2022)—shows how public design can constrain private capture. The limitation, however, is that Pix remains national. Its architecture does not resolve cross-border coordination problems where standards bodies operate without democratic mandate. Thus, resistance to capture often flourishes locally but struggles globally.

A broader implication follows. The tension between decentralisation and capture cannot be solved once, in code. It must be managed continuously, in governance. Systems need renewal. They need rotation of authority, transparent processes for dispute resolution, and mechanisms for rewriting rules that do not rely on single points of influence. Without these safeguards, decentralised networks risk becoming the linguistic veneer of a familiar hierarchy.

As the future of digital money unfolds, the questions sharpen. Who should define wallet standards? Who should run identity directories? Who should maintain the protocols that settle value across continents? The answers will determine not just efficiency or security, but the distribution of power itself. Capture is not a defect. It is a force. And unless institutions and communities learn how to counter it, the rails of tomorrow may look remarkably like the rails of yesterday—only hidden beneath new code.

Commons Pathway: If users hold keys and institutions provide services, pluralism grows. Civic skills and new governance experiments are required

In April 2021, in Oslo, the Norwegian government released its report on the country's first municipal experiment using blockchain-based land registries. The pilot was modest—a few hundred parcels, a limited administrative remit—but one detail mattered more than the headlines: citizens, not officials, held the cryptographic keys that authorised updates to their property records. The registry still relied on public institutions for audit, dispute resolution, and archival durability, yet the authority to initiate a change rested with individuals. There was no password-reset desk. No single administrator could override a citizen's entry without a public record of the attempt. A subtle reordering occurred. The custodians became service providers rather than gatekeepers. A quiet shift began where the locus of power sat.

That shift captures the essence of the commons pathway: decentralisation not as ideology, but as muscle memory. The Oslo trial did not claim to revolutionise property rights. Its achievement was simpler and more significant. It demonstrated that when individuals hold the keys to their digital assets—or their digital identities—institutions change role. They become coordinators rather than controllers, adjudicators rather than owners of the ledger. And when the distribution of authority changes, the distribution of responsibility changes with it. This is the challenge and promise of a commons: it enlarges the space where citizens act, but demands civic skill to sustain what it grants. *A shared system only works if its stewards know they are stewards.*

The first claim follows from a visible pattern. Show: in 2020, Buenos Aires' open-source initiative to digitise social-benefit disbursements used non-custodial wallets accessible from low-cost Android phones. Name: the city's Secretariat of Innovation led the pilot and worked with local developer groups to ensure recipients controlled their keys. Explain: this design choice mattered because beneficiaries were historically dependent on intermediaries who released funds on timetables that often shifted at short notice. When keys moved to users, a behavioural change occurred: household budgeting stabilised, and fraud reports fell because tampering required physical access to the device or consent from the owner. Implication: where autonomy expands, vulnerability can shrink—provided the surrounding structures support users rather than replace them.

A second example highlights how pluralism grows when institutions provide services without seizing control. Show: in 2016, the Government of Estonia extended its e-Residency programme to include non-custodial signing keys for company formation and digital identity. Name: Estonia's Information System Authority (RIA) implemented this through its decentralised X-Road architecture. Explain: e-Residents could register firms, sign documents, and access cross-border business services while retaining cryptographic control over their identity credentials. The state verified the identity but did not hold the keys. Implication: even when institutions remain strong, they can design themselves to be infrastructure, not overlords. The commons expands without eroding state capability.

Yet a credible counter-example warns that autonomy alone is insufficient. Show: in 2022, during Nigeria's push to migrate public payments to the eNaira infrastructure, many users abandoned self-managed wallets because key recovery was confusing and customer support was inconsistent. Name: the Central Bank of Nigeria's rollout. Explain: when the cognitive load is high and the educational scaffolding is thin, people gravitate back to custodial intermediaries who promise predictability. Implication: without civic skill and user education, autonomy can be a burden, not an empowerment. The commons becomes a maze rather than a platform.

Reconciling these examples reveals the motif threading through all decentralised systems: *a shared system only works if its stewards know they are stewards.* Technology can distribute control; only practice can distribute competence. And competence is uneven without deliberate investment. Civic skill is not ornamental. It is operational.

For the commons pathway to take root, three visible behaviours matter more than rhetoric. The first is the willingness of institutions to provide infrastructure without demanding custody. If a bank offers a key-signing service but keeps the keys itself, it has re-centralised the system in everything but name. Evidence of sincerity lies in metrics: how many users hold their own keys, how often signature requests bypass institutional servers, and how transparent the service is about its operational boundaries.

The second behaviour concerns decision-making. Distributed systems can only remain plural if governance avoids concentration. Show: in 2021, Gitcoin DAO experimented with quadratic funding for public goods, allowing thousands of small contributors to influence grant distribution more than a few wealthy donors could. Name: Gitcoin DAO, rooted in Denver's early Ethereum community. Explain: the mechanism amplified broad participation and limited the impact of concentrated capital. Implication: governance innovations matter because they can prevent systems from sliding back toward oligarchy even when participation scales.

The third behaviour is education. Commons do not sustain themselves without an informed public. Infrastructure requires institutional competence; decentralisation requires social competence. When users know how to rotate keys, how to verify signatures, how to spot malicious updates, the system gains resilience. Behaviour becomes the first line of defence.

These strands intertwine around a deeper question: what does it mean for a financial or informational network to be a commons? Not merely that it is open-source, or permissionless, or non-custodial. Those are technical properties. A commons exists when the distribution of control aligns with a distribution of responsibility. It is political. It is cultural. It is pedagogical. And it demands governance that evolves without ossifying.

The implications ripple into institutional design. A bank that offers key-management assistance can operate as a support actor, measured by how many users "graduate" to secure self-custody after using its guidance tools. A regulator can set standards that require interoperability without mandating custodial choke points, using audit trails rather than asset control to maintain compliance. A fintech provider can adopt multi-party computation (MPC) that lets users co-sign transactions without revealing their keys, balancing security with autonomy. Each of these choices shifts the system closer to a commons rather than a hierarchy.

Still, the commons pathway remains fragile. Standards bodies may drift toward centralisation if participation narrows. Wallet software may consolidate, turning a handful of interfaces into the effective governors of user experience. And communities may tire of the burdens of self-governance, preferring the relief of delegation. Pluralism shrinks whenever convenience eclipses agency.

But the pathway is not naïve. It acknowledges trade-offs and risks while insisting that agency can scale if design and education move together. The governance experiments emerging in Seoul, Reykjavik, and Nairobi—where community groups test participatory budgeting, verified credentials, and shared digital registries—show that digital commons can coexist with strong institutions. Their common feature is not technology. It is intention. A commitment to treat citizens as capable actors rather than passive recipients.

As digital money matures, the unresolved tension crystallises: how much autonomy do users genuinely want, and how much responsibility are they willing to carry? The commons pathway offers pluralism, resilience, and a distribution of power that mirrors democratic ideals. But it asks something in return: practice. Skills. Engagement. The willingness to be a steward rather than a customer. The next phase of monetary design will not be determined by infrastructure alone. It will be shaped by whether societies choose to cultivate the civic competence needed to hold their own keys—literally and figuratively—and whether institutions choose to support that competence rather than displace it.

Choosing a Monetary Citizenship: Heuristics to navigate: follow incentives, test exit options, demand transparency. A checklist translates theory into daily choices

In February 2023, in Beirut, a crowd formed outside the Hamra Branch of Bank Audi after the institution imposed an unannounced withdrawal cap. Tempers frayed when a man named Karim, a local café owner, arrived with a court order permitting him to access his own deposits. The branch manager declined to honour it. Police were called. By dusk, the street hummed with a bitter paradox: the money was unquestionably his, yet the practical ability to use it resided elsewhere. A type of citizenship—monetary citizenship—had been revoked without process. People watched, murmuring versions of the same question. If one cannot rely on the institutions that hold their savings, what, precisely, does monetary belonging mean?

The episode was not unique to Lebanon, nor was its logic confined to crisis economies. In December 2013, during Cyprus's bank restructuring, depositors discovered that their claims were subordinate to institutional solvency. In both cases, the legal guarantees remained on paper; the operational guarantees dissolved at the counter. Monetary citizenship, it turned out, was not solely a matter of what the law promised but of what the system permitted. Karim's frustration captured the difference. Rights without exit, rights without transparency, and rights without institutional accountability behave more like permissions than entitlements. Five words echo in such moments: *Who actually controls your money?*

That question is not rhetorical. It is diagnostic. It is the first step in choosing a monetary citizenship—an orientation to the institutions, rails, and networks through which one's economic life flows. The term may sound abstract, but it is anchored in the most concrete of behaviours: who holds the keys, who sets the fees, who controls settlement windows, who determines whether a transfer goes through. Monetary citizenship is enacted in seconds, not speeches.

Show. In 2021, during Argentina's inflation spike, a Buenos Aires teacher named Lucía began splitting her monthly salary across three buckets: pesos for groceries, a small bitcoin allocation held in a non-custodial wallet, and a USDT balance stored with a custodial exchange. Name. Data from Argentina's National Institute of Statistics and Census (INDEC, 2021) recorded consumer price inflation exceeding 50 per cent year-on-year. Explain. Lucía discovered that each bucket offered different levels of autonomy, risk, and visibility. The pesos were liquid but melting. The USDT balance was stable but subordinate to the exchange's operational discretion. The self-custodied bitcoin was volatile yet immune to withdrawal caps. Implication. Her pattern revealed the first heuristic of monetary citizenship: follow incentives. Systems reward behaviours aligned with their design; they punish behaviours that contradict it.

Following incentives requires more than economic intuition. It demands attention to institutional posture. A bank that earns revenue from transaction fees and deposit spreads has incentives to retain customer funds, discourage swift movement, and manage liquidity through predictable flows. A decentralised protocol that earns security from distributed participation has incentives to keep exits cheap, keep entry open, and keep the rules consistent. A custodial stablecoin issuer has incentives tied to regulatory scrutiny, which may prioritise safety over user autonomy. When people ignore these incentives, they misinterpret the behaviours of institutions as moral failings rather than structural features. Monetary citizenship begins with recognising structure.

The second heuristic—test exit options—emerges from a different kind of scene. Show. In September 2022, the Kenyan platform M-Pesa suffered a multi-hour outage that interrupted payments for millions. Name. Safaricom, the operator, issued a public apology and restored service by evening. Explain. For many users, it was the first time they experienced a system that was both indispensable and irreplaceable. There was no alternative rail with equal reach. The outage became a stress test for exit. The absence of an alternative rail transformed a technical failure into a political moment. Implication. In any monetary system, exit is the ultimate backstop—not protest, not rhetoric, but the ability to move one's value elsewhere without obstruction.

Exit options can be measured. They vary by jurisdiction, infrastructure, and governance. In the United Kingdom, the Current Account Switch Service allows bank customers to migrate accounts within seven working days. In contrast, in parts of West Africa, mobile money users can switch providers only by physically cashing out one balance and re-loading another, exposing them to fees and security risks. The visibility of exit costs indicates the degree of power concentration. A system that supports true exit makes the cost of leaving low and the process predictable. A system that fears exit introduces friction—delays, paperwork, validation loops, or unexplained failures.

Yet a counter-example must be confronted. Show. In early 2020, during the onset of the COVID-19 pandemic, many Italian banks temporarily lifted transfer limits and accelerated settlement to facilitate emergency payments. Name. Italy's Treasury and the Bank of Italy coordinated these measures. Explain. Even highly centralised systems can support flexible exit under pressure. Implication. Exit is not solely a property of decentralised systems; it is a property of institutional willingness. Testing exit is as much about observing behaviour during stress as examining rules on paper.

The third heuristic—demand transparency—threads through both incentives and exit. It concerns visibility: how clearly one can see who holds what power, under which conditions, and with which constraints. Show. In 2018, the European Commission mandated stronger reporting rules for Payment Services Providers under PSD2, requiring data portability and clearer disclosures. Name. PSD2 (EU, 2018). Explain. Transparency enabled challenger banks to compete because users could verify fees, authorisation flows, and security practices. Implication. Without transparency, power hides in the plumbing.

Transparency is measurable: what logs are available, what audit trails exist, what metrics are public. A decentralised protocol with open-source code offers one form. A regulated bank with audited financials offers another. What matters is whether the user can verify claims rather than rely on trust alone. Transparency transforms monetary citizenship from passive reliance into active oversight.

Threaded through these heuristics is a motif: *agency requires verification*. It appears in Karim's frustration; it appears in Lucía's allocation; it appears in the M-Pesa outage. Verification is the connective tissue of monetary citizenship. It turns economic life from dependence into participation.

To operationalise the idea, consider how each heuristic plays out in daily choices. Following incentives becomes a habit: noticing when promotional rates mask illiquid commitments; recognising when a "free" service monetises one's data; understanding that a custodial wallet's convenience carries the incentive of retaining user balances. Testing exit becomes a periodic ritual: attempting small transfers across rails, checking withdrawal limits during quiet periods, observing which services introduce new friction without explanation.

Demanding transparency becomes a discipline: reading status pages, monitoring fee changes, noting whether customer service responses match public policy.

Examples from beyond crisis contexts show how these behaviours scale. Show. In 2017, the Monetary Authority of Singapore (MAS) launched its Open Banking initiative, encouraging APIs that allowed customers to export transaction histories and integrate them into third-party budgeting apps. Name. MAS, Singapore, 2017. Explain. Users gained a clearer sense of how institutions handled their data, enabling them to choose providers whose practices aligned with their preferences. Implication. When transparency expands, competition shifts from branding to behaviour.

Show. In 2022, Brazil's Pix instant payments system reached over 140 million users, according to Banco Central do Brasil. Name. Banco Central do Brasil, Pix, 2022. Explain. Pix offered free real-time transfers across institutions, reducing exit friction and challenging traditional banks to improve services. Implication. When exit becomes cheap, institutions must compete on value, not lock-in.

A limitation, however, must be acknowledged. Some systems appear transparent yet obscure the most consequential layers. Show. In 2021, several centralised crypto exchanges boasted real-time "proof-of-reserves" dashboards. Name. Binance and Kraken released public attestations. Explain. While useful, these proofs did not reveal liabilities, operational risk, or rehypothecation practices. Implication. Transparency can be partial, performative, or strategically selective; therefore, users must evaluate not merely what is disclosed, but what remains concealed.

Reconciling these threads leads to a deeper understanding: monetary citizenship is not about choosing a particular asset or rail. It is about forming a literacy of power—how it is exercised, how it is constrained, and how it can be exited. It is a stance rather than a subscription.

This stance has three visible consequences. First, it pushes institutions to treat users as partners rather than passive accounts. A bank that anticipates exit strengthens its offerings. A protocol that anticipates scrutiny improves its governance. Second, it anchors autonomy in practice rather than ideology. Monetary citizenship is enacted by actions—moving funds, verifying claims, maintaining keys—not just beliefs. Third, it reframes financial responsibility. Users cease being customers alone; they become participants with rights they must assert.

The motif returns: *agency requires verification*. It is the quiet discipline that sustains pluralism.

The unresolved tension sits at the centre of this subchapter. How far should individuals go in exercising monetary citizenship, and how far should institutions go in supporting it? Too much autonomy may overwhelm users; too much paternalism may erode agency. The balance is neither fixed nor universal. It must be negotiated—through incentives, through exit, and through transparency.

The forward test for the reader is simple, yet demanding. Which systems around you reveal their incentives openly? Which allow you to leave at low cost and without obstruction? Which provide transparency deep enough to verify rather than trust? Monetary citizenship is not a label granted by a state or a protocol. It is a practice one cultivates, choice by choice, system by system, until the act of verifying becomes as instinctive as the act of earning.

About the Author

Mateo Quiral writes about money as a system of power and trust. He has spent a decade interviewing technologists, policy thinkers, and bankers across several continents, listening for where incentives align or collide. His work follows a simple question: who benefits when money moves, and who is left carrying risk. Raised between Mediterranean trading cities, he learned early that exchange is a cultural story as much as a ledger entry. Quiral's reporting blends historical vignettes with clear explanations of complex mechanisms, aiming to give readers judgement rather than jargon. He believes financial literacy should include civic literacy: understanding how rules, networks, and institutions shape our everyday autonomy. This book continues that mission, showing how a stateless protocol and centuries-old banking practices are reshaping each other, and why ordinary users deserve a seat at the table.

www.ingramcontent.com/pod-product-compliance
Lightning Source LLC
Chambersburg PA
CBHW031343230926
51848CB00002B/364
* 9 7 8 9 3 7 4 5 9 5 7 0 1 *